Designing Data Reports that Work

Designing Data Reports that Work provides research-based best practices for constructing effective data systems in schools and for designing reports that are relevant, necessary, and easily understood. Clear and coherent data systems and data reports significantly improve educators' data use and save educators time and frustration. The strategies in this book will help those responsible for designing education data reports—including school leaders, administrators, and educational technology vendors—to create productive data reports individualized for each school or district. This book breaks down the key concepts in creating and implementing data systems, ensuring that you are a better partner with teachers and staff so they can work with and use data correctly and improve teaching and learning.

Jenny Grant Rankin, Ph.D., teaches at the University of Cambridge for the PostDoc Masterclass and is the former Chief Education and Research Officer at Illuminate Education, an educational technology data systems company. She has been an award-winning teacher, technology coordinator, site administrator, and district administrator.

Other Eye On Education Books
Available from Routledge
(www.routledge.com/eyeoneducation)

How to Make Data Work: A Guide for Educational Leaders
Jenny Grant Rankin

Mentoring is a Verb: Strategies for Improving College and Career Readiness
Russ Olwell

A School Leaders Guide to Implementing the Common Core: Inclusive Practices for All Students
Gloria Campbell-Whatley, Dawson Hancock, and David M. Dunaway

What Connected Educators Do Differently
Todd Whitaker, Jeffrey Zoul, and Jimmy Casas

BRAVO Principal! Building Relationships with Actions that Value Others, 2nd Edition
Sandra Harris

Get Organized! Time Management for School Leaders, 2nd Edition
Frank Buck

The Educator's Guide to Writing a Book: Practical Advice for Teachers and Leaders
Cathie E. West

Data, Data Everywhere: Bringing All The Data Together for Continuous School Improvement, 2nd edition
Victoria Bernhardt

Leading Learning for Digital Natives: Combining Data and Technology in the Classroom
Rebecca J. Blink

The Trust Factor: Strategies for School Leaders
Julie Peterson Combs, Stacey Edmonson, and Sandra Harris

The Assistant Principal's Guide: New Strategies for New Responsibilities
M. Scott Norton

The Principal as Human Resources Leader: A Guide to Exemplary Practices for Personnel Administration
M. Scott Norton

Formative Assessment Leadership: Identify, Plan, Apply, Assess, Refine
Karen L. Sanzo, Steve Myran, and John Caggiano

Easy and Effective Professional Development: The Power of Peer Observation to Improve Teaching
Catherine Beck, Paul D'Elia, and Michael W. Lamond

Job-Embedded Professional Development: Support, Collaboration, and Learning in Schools
Sally J. Zepeda

Leading Schools in an Era of Declining Resources
J. Howard Johnston and Ronald Williamson

Creating Safe Schools: A Guide for School Leaders, Teachers, and Parents
Franklin P. Schargel

Designing Data Reports that Work

A Guide for Creating Data Systems in Schools and Districts

Jenny Grant Rankin

NEW YORK AND LONDON

First published 2016
by Routledge
711 Third Avenue, New York, NY 10017

and by Routledge
2 Park Square, Milton Park, Abingdon, Oxon, OX14 4RN

Routledge is an imprint of the Taylor & Francis Group, an informa business

© 2016 Taylor & Francis

The right of Jenny Grant Rankin to be identified as author of this work
has been asserted by her in accordance with sections 77 and 78 of the
Copyright, Designs and Patents Act 1988.

All rights reserved. No part of this book may be reprinted or
reproduced or utilized in any form or by any electronic, mechanical,
or other means, now known or hereafter invented, including photocopying
and recording, or in any information storage or retrieval system,
without permission in writing from the publishers.

Trademark notice: Product or corporate names may be trademarks or
registered trademarks, and are used only for identification and explanation
without intent to infringe.

Library of Congress Cataloging-in-Publication Data
Names: Rankin, Jenny Grant, author.
Title: Designing data reports that work: a guide for creating data systems
in schools and districts/by Jenny Grant Rankin.
Description: New York, NY: Routledge, 2016. |
Includes bibliographical references.
Identifiers: LCCN 2015034069| ISBN 9781138956179 (hardback) |
ISBN 9781138956186 (pbk.) | ISBN 9781315665849 (ebook)
Subjects: LCSH: Educational evaluation—Data processing. | Educational indicators.
Classification: LCC LB2822.75 .R359 2016 | DDC 379.1/580285—dc23
LC record available at http://lccn.loc.gov/2015034069

ISBN: 978-1-138-95617-9 (hbk)
ISBN: 978-1-138-95618-6 (pbk)
ISBN: 978-1-315-66584-9 (ebk)

Typeset in Optima
by Florence Production Ltd, Stoodleigh, Devon, UK

This book is dedicated to
Lane D. Rankin.
You are my hero in so many ways.

Contents

Preface   x
Acknowledgments   xiii
Meet the Author   xvi
eResources   xix

1 **Data Reports Are the Silent Star**   1
   The Data Analysis Error Epidemic   1
   Educators Cannot Maximize Data without Data Reports that Work   2
   Educators Are Primed for Good Data Use   3
   Effective Data Reporting Is Often the Missing Ingredient   4
   It Is up to You to Help   7
   Over-the-Counter Data = Data that Works   8
   Everyone Benefits, Including You   10
   References   10

2 **Label Standards**   14
   Definition of Label   14
   How to Implement Label Standards   15
   Titles   17
   Footers   32
   References   42

3 **Supplemental Documentation Standards**   43
   Definition of Supplemental Documentation   43
   How to Implement Supplemental Documentation Standards   44
   Reference Sheets   45

vii

Contents

Reference Guides 51
References 59

4 Help System Standards   **60**
Definition of Help System 60
How to Implement Help System Standards 61
Tech Lessons (Using the System) 63
Data Analysis Lessons 82
References 90

5 Package/Display Standards: Big Picture   **91**
Definition of Package/Display 91
How to Implement Package/Display Standards 92
Credibility 94
References 102

6 Package/Display Standards: Report Design   **103**
Report Design Aspects 103
Key Features 103
Design 120
References 145

7 Package/Display Standards: User Interface   **148**
User Interface Aspects 148
Navigation 148
Input Controls 162
References 174

8 Content Standards   **175**
Definition of Content 175
How to Implement Effective Content 176
Each Report 177
Report Suite 180
References 203

9 Work with Educators   **204**
Communication 204
Respect Data Users' Expertise 208
Troubleshooting 209
A "Lean in" Culture 210
References 212

10 Put It All Together 213

"Big Picture" Action Table 213
Help for the Overwhelmed 214
Final Words 215
Reference 217

Preface

The data systems and data reports educators use to view and analyze data have a significant impact on the success of educators' data use. Improved data tools make educators' other efforts to improve data use—such as training and staff supports—go further and be needed on a reduced scale. Extensive research has informed data reporting standards for the best ways to report data to educators. This book guides readers in how to implement those standards within any data tools readers design or create for educators.

> Standards shared in this book have been shown to improve educators' data analyses by up to 436 percent.

Audience

This book is for edtech providers, educator leaders, or other stakeholders who present or display data for educators. For example, you might provide any of these:

- data reports (either within your data system or by exporting data and constructing supplementary reports with another tool);
- data system(s);
- edtech product(s) with a feedback/data component.

You might be based at a company that sells edtech, or you might be based at a school district or organization that provides data tools for its own use or others' use. In this book you will often be referred to as a data system/report provider (DSRP).

Book Structure and Content

The next seven chapters will help you identify and overcome shortcomings in the data system, reports, and/or tools you provide to educators. Each chapter will provide the following for one of the five over-the-counter data (OTCD) components:

- **Description** of the component and what it looks like in a reporting environment;
- **Summary** of how to implement the component within your data system/reports;
- **Standard-based lessons for implementing** the component (including illustrations, before and after examples, templates, etc.).

Standards are numbered according to their component, subcomponent, and standard. For example, Standard 1.2.01 is numbered that way because "1." at the beginning refers to the first OTCD Standard component (Label), "2." in the middle refers to the second Label subcomponent (Footers), and "01" at the end refers to the actual standard (Present). Thus Standard 1.2.01 relates to labels—more specifically footers—being present in the data reporting environment.

Recommendations Are Research-Based

 The Over-the-Counter Data (OTCD) Standards taught in this book synthesize more than 300 studies and texts from experts in the field. See online details on a summary of this research.

Benefits

Following the lessons in this book will likely result in reduced workload for those supporting educators with data use. Applying the book's concepts will improve your data systems/reports so they actively improve data use, save educators' time, and reduce educators' frustration. This book will help you make data reports that work for those who view and use them, so educators are better able to help students.

Acknowledgments

The research that went into this book was accompanied by a career learning the topic's intricacies and putting data reporting and data use into practice. I thus owe deep gratitude to the educators who oversaw these experiences, and the staff at the sites where it took place. These include Buena Park Junior High School under Debra Diaz's leadership; Orangeview Junior High School under Dr. Kevin Astor's leadership; Saddleback Valley Unified School District under Dr. Kathy Dick's leadership (with additional accolades going to Margaret Stewart, my unparalleled secretary at the time and a data whiz in her own right, as well as the supportive JL4 team); and Illuminate Education under Lane Rankin's leadership. Each of these individuals is a prime example of how strong data leadership benefits educators, those who report data to educators, and—especially—students. I am also very grateful to the professionals who lent their wisdom to the book in the form of chapter vignettes. These include Leo Bialis-White, Vice President of Impact at Schoolzilla; Dr. Margie Johnson, Business Intelligence Coordinator of Metropolitan Nashville Public Schools; Rudi Lewis, Chief Operating Officer of Silverback Learning Solutions; Lane Rankin, CEO/Founder of Illuminate Education; Rufus Thompson, Implementation Manager at Illuminate Education and former Technology Coordinator for Mountain View School District in Ontario, California; and Ryan Winter, President of LinkIt!. When my quantitative study on this book's standards concluded and I sent findings to the nearly 100 edtech data system providers (including edtech with data components) in the U.S., these individuals were those who showed the most interest in applying research-based concepts to data tools in order to best help educators and students. They serve as examples of the ethics, thoughtfulness, and wisdom we wish upon all edtech

Acknowledgments

providers in order to best serve stakeholders. I thank Ann Barreto, as well, for being so kind as to review the book in its early stages and offer helpful feedback. I am grateful to the incomparable educators who reviewed the book and offered their endorsements. These include Dr. Margie Johnson, Lane Rankin, and Rufus Thompson. I owe additional thanks to Rufus Thompson, along with Dr. Gail Thompson, for their mentorship and continual encouragement. Whenever my steam threatened to wane, these bosses inspired me to persist, and I am continually inspired by them. I also owe additional thanks to Dr. Margie Johnson for her support with whatever I needed from the beginning—when this book was just forming—and through to the end. Her early involvement in implementing OTCD Standards is testament to the kind of educator she is: aware of what is needed even before the rest of the field catches up. I thank Dr. Darrell Passwater for being a valued mentor whose advice helped me focus on what matters most. Steve Rees of School Wise Press also receives my gratitude for sharing valued resources and dialogue on this topic. I also thank my daughter, Piper Rankin, for her understanding whenever Mommy was on her laptop again. Her five years of life have all seen me stealing time for this book, and I look forward to celebrating its completion with her. Equally understanding was my husband, Lane Rankin, whom I thank for believing in the project's importance and supporting me with love. I am so blessed to have such a wonderful partner in life. I also appreciate that Lane granted use of screenshots from Illuminate's data systems and help system. Greg DeVore (CEO and Co-Founder of Blue Mango Learning Systems) kindly provided details used when describing the ScreenSteps-created help system, as well as permission to use ScreenSteps images. I thank my sons—Clyde Rankin, Zach Rankin, and Tyler Rankin (who lend their genius to the data edtech field)—and friends for always being so positive when I spoke of my research and this book. The same goes for my mother, Nancy Grant, who is my unwavering rock of encouragement and love (and the "Gammy time" with Piper sure helped the book's progress). I also thank Michael Walker for kindly providing my author photo (a great photographer who gets it on the first try). In addition, I owe special thanks to Heather Jarrow, my amazing editor at Routledge/Taylor & Francis Group. Enthusiastic from the start, Heather was the key to this dream of mine coming true. None of the many books available on educator data use are devoted to the crucial role of the data tools that educators use, yet Heather was not scared off from

Acknowledgments

this lack of convention. Rather, she saw the need for it, provided sage advice, and helped the book become a tool for change. I also thank Karen Adler, an editorial assistant at Routledge/Taylor & Francis Group, for answering my many questions in such a welcoming way. I feel so blessed to have been helped by the caring souls acknowledged here.

Meet the Author

Award-winning educator Dr. Jenny Grant Rankin, who teaches at the University of Cambridge for the PostDoc Masterclass, has a Ph.D. in Education featuring a specialization in School Improvement Leadership. She is an active member of Mensa and many educational organizations, particularly within the areas of data, assessment, and technology.

After working in higher education overseeing a university's Visual Arts and Information Technology Departments, Dr. Rankin pursued a rewarding career in K-12 public education. She served as a teacher (of junior high school English, Newspaper, and AVID), teacher on special assignment (TOSA) and technology coordinator, junior high school assistant principal, district administrator (overseeing assessment and data use for a 35,000-

student school district) and chief education and research officer (CERO) for Illuminate Education (an educational technology data systems company where she was able to impact data use at hundreds of school districts across the U.S.).

Dr. Rankin's books relate to data, education, and technology. Her papers and articles on this book's topic have appeared in such publications as ASCD's *Educational Leadership, CCNews: Newsletter of the California Council on Teacher Education (CCTE), EdCircuit, Ed-Fi Alliance Blog, EdSurge* (funded by *The Washington Post*), *EdTech Review, Edtech Women, Edukwest, eSchoolNews, International Society for Technology in Education (ISTE) EdTechHub*, and *OnCUE: Journal of Computer Using Educators (CUE)*. Dr. Rankin's work has also appeared in the *Mensa Bulletin* and conference proceedings.

Dr. Rankin has given a TED Talk on this topic at TEDxTUM and presents this research annually at the U.S. Department of Education's Institute of Education Sciences (IES) National Center for Education Statistics (NCES) STATS-DC Conferences and at the International Society for Technology in Education (ISTE) Conference. She also presented on this topic at the American Educational Research Association (AERA) Annual Meeting; California Council on Teacher Education (CCTE) Conference; California Educational Research Association (CERA) Conferences; Carnegie Foundation Summit on Improvement in Education; Classroom 2.0's Learning 2.0 Conference; Connect: Canada's National Learning and Technology Conference; K-12 Online Conference; Learning Revolution Conference; Leadership Innovation Event at Montfort College, Chang Mai, Thailand; National Council on Measurement in Education (NCME) Annual Meeting; OZeLIVE! Australia: Ed Tech Down Under Conference; Society for Information Technology & Teacher Education (SITE) Conferences; Technology Information Center for Administrative Leadership (TICAL) School Leadership Summit; University of California, Irvine (UCI) Digital Learning Lab; University of California, Los Angeles (UCLA) and National Center for Research on Evaluation, Standards, and Student Testing (CRESST) Conference; and others.

Winning Teacher of the Year was a favorite honor, as was having the U.S. flag flown over the United States Capitol at the request of the Honorable Christopher Cox, U.S. Representative, in recognition of Dr. Rankin's dedication to her students. Her more recent awards include the #EduWin Award, EdTech's 2014 Must-Read Higher Education Technology Blogs List, finalist for EdTech Digest's Trendsetter Award, SIGNL Award for

Twitter Followers Momentum, and Association for the Advancement of Computing in Education (AACE) Academic Expert. Her research website is also included on MIT's concise List of EdTech Blogs and Sites.

Dr. Rankin has served as judge for the University of Pennsylvania Graduate School of Education's prestigious Milken-Penn Graduate School of Education Business Plan Competitions and the California Student Media Festivals (CSMF) sponsored by PBS SoCAL, Computer Using Educators (CUE), and Discovery Education. Dr. Rankin was also paid to examine alignment issues related to the Common Core State Standards (CCSS) summative assessments as part of the Smarter Balanced Assessment Consortium (SBAC) Alignment Study, and she also served on the Smarter Balanced Assessment Consortium (SBAC) Panel for Achievement Level Setting.

In addition, Dr. Rankin has served on research committees for the International Society for Technology in Education (ISTE), the Society for Information Technology & Teacher Education (SITE), and the California Council on Teacher Education (CCTE). She also served on the Panel of Experts and the Advisory Board for the New Media Consortium (NMC) Horizon Report: 2015 K12 Edition, honored with a special listing and acknowledgment in the report. Dr. Rankin also served as reviewer for the *Handbook of Research on Innovations in Information Retrieval, Analysis, and Management* from IGI Global and is an expert reviewer (reviewing for the journal *Educational Researcher* and multiple awards) for the American Educational Research Association (AERA). She regularly shares new research on this book's topic at www.overthecounterdata.com and https://twitter.com/OTCData (Twitter handle @OTCData).

eResources

Keep an eye out for the eResources icon throughout this book, which indicates a resource is available online. Many of the tools in this book can be downloaded, printed, used to copy/paste text, and/or manipulated to suit your individualized use. You can access these downloads by visiting the book product page on our website: www.routledge.com/products/9781138956186. Then click on the tab that reads "eResources" and then select the file(s) you need. The file(s) will download directly to your computer.

Tool

- OTCD Standards
- Details on Evidence (supporting every one of the OTCD Standards)
- Needs Matrix (there are both pdf and xlsx versions)
- Sample Data Types to Support Data Analyses
- Sample Questions Data Can Help Answer
- Reference Sheet Templates (there are both doc and docx versions)
- Reference Guide Templates (there are both doc and docx versions)
- Sample Reference Sheets
- Sample Reference Guides
- Sample Help Lesson from Illuminate Education

eResources

- Report Before and After Examples
- Common Inappropriate Data Displays
- Input Control Examples
- Evaluation of Data Tool in Online Survey Format
- Dilemma Countered by Proactive Mindset Table
- Big Picture Action Table
- Glossary

Data Reports Are the Silent Star

The Data Analysis Error Epidemic

The National Center for Education Statistics estimates less than 2 percent of school districts in the U.S. are able to turn data[1] into information educators can actually use (Sparks, 2014). Worse, educators who do use data typically use it incorrectly. In national studies of districts known for strong data use, teachers showed difficulty with question posing, data comprehension, and data interpretation, answering only 48 percent of questions correctly when drawing inferences from given data (U.S. Department of Education Office of Planning, Evaluation and Policy Development [USDEOPEPD], 2009, 2011).

That occurred at the nation's top data-using districts, whereas educators' data use elsewhere is worse. For example, in a quantitative study involving 211 educators of varied backgrounds and roles, participants averaged 11 percent correct when answering basic analysis questions about given data (Rankin, 2013). This latter study took place in California, where multiple state assessments have a history of rendering data that is difficult to understand. Many studies rendered similar findings: educators use data to inform decisions, but they commonly misunderstand the data. Whether data-using conditions are ideal or not, an accuracy range of 11–48 percent when educators use data is alarming.

Here is a synopsis of how educators' data-informed decision-making impacts students:

View/Analyze Reports	**Make Decisions**	**Impact Students**
• 44% of educators use data systems directly, but the majority view printed versions of reports others generate for them (Underwood et al., 2008). • As noted earlier, only 11–48% of educators' data interpretations are accurate.	• Educators then make decisions informed by their understanding of the data. • If educators are not making appropriate data analyses, they are not likely making appropriate decisions guided by those flawed analyses.	• Educators' data-informed decisions impact students (as the main reason they are being made is to impact students). • Decisions based on flawed data analyses are likely to negatively impact students.

Figure 1.1

Educators Cannot Maximize Data without Data Reports that Work

Most literature and dialogue in education communities mistakenly treats data misunderstandings as if they are educators' fault. If educators really were to blame, it would be within educators' power to entirely remedy data problems. However, even when educators implement recommended interventions with fidelity, this is not possible.

For example, professional development (PD) and staffing-based supports such as strong leadership, data coaches, professional learning communities (PLCs), and collaboration hold great potential to improve educators' data use, and most districts already utilize them on some level. However, many findings indicate PD and staff supports are not omnipotent. In other words, while they *are* beneficial and recommended, they will *not* bring a 100 percent accuracy rate to educators' data analyses. For example:

- Many districts cannot give schools the amount of PD they need; PD might not always be available locally due to budget cuts, and developing PD resources on their own is too expensive an option for schools and districts (Kidron, 2012).

- In a study where teachers received PD in educational measurement/ assessment, *all* teachers struggled afterwards with statistical terms and measurement concepts (Zapata-Rivera & VanWinkle, 2010).

- A report prepared for IES by Regional Educational Laboratory Midwest confirmed the limitations of the most popular data analysis supports in school districts, noting data staff and training resources can be limited at the local level, as is staff with proper data analysis experience and skills at the state level (McDonald et al., 2007).

- Teacher coaches can stop coaching teachers as the school year progresses due to other responsibilities (Underwood et al., 2008).

> "Minimize the extent to which [educators] need to actively analyze data. ... We give such tools to physicians and military decision makers; education is no less complex and no less important."
>
> U.S. Department of Education Office of Educational Technology, 2012, p. 49

- Expecting educators to be dependent on on-site data system experts for help to colleagues causes problems and creates a bottleneck and can leave support staff overworked (Wayman et al., 2007).

Even educators employing PD and staffing-based supports with fidelity cannot solve the data analysis error epidemic on their own. Educator-implemented interventions can improve educators' data use, but they can only help to some degree.

Educators Are Primed for Good Data Use

Those providing data systems and/or data reports to educators have been given some favorable circumstances with which to work. Though no one is perfect, as is no teacher preparation program, consider how ideal educators generally are as a client- or user-base. Educators are primed for good data use in that they are:

- **highly skilled**—e.g., 95 percent of teachers are considered "highly qualified" by No Child Left Behind (NCLB) standards (American Institutes for Research, 2013);

- **well educated**—e.g., 99 percent of American teachers have bachelor's degrees, 48 percent have master's degrees, and over 7 percent have more advanced graduate degrees (Papay, Harvard Graduate School of Education, 2007);
- **intelligent**—e.g., educators have above-average IQs;[2]
- **care about students**—e.g., 85 percent of teachers say they became teachers because they wanted to make a difference in children's lives (Bill and Melinda Gates Foundation, 2014), and 90 percent of students believe their teachers care about their learning (Northwest Evaluation Association, 2014);
- **embracing data use**—e.g., most educators are eager to analyze and then act on the data they see (Hattie, 2010; van der Meij, 2008);
- **embracing technology use**—e.g., teachers indicated overwhelming support for using technology to improve learning, and 85 percent of teachers reported daily use of technology to support teaching (Bill and Melinda Gates Foundation, 2012);
- **employing approaches within their power to grow professionally**—e.g., districts devote 1 percent to 8 percent of their operating budgets to providing professional learning (Killion & Hirsh, 2012); the quality of training and supports can always be improved, but at least some is taking place.

With such highly qualified and proactive individuals making so many data analysis errors even at districts known for strong data PD, staff, and culture, educator-implemented data analysis interventions are clearly not enough. It is important to consider and remedy problems with the reporting tools educators are using.

Effective Data Reporting Is Often the Missing Ingredient

Providing a data system designed specifically for users' needs is more effective than expecting training to get users as prepared as they need to be to use the system and its data (Underwood et al. 2008). Expecting educators to improve data use while using ineffective or marginally effective data tools is misguided.

In education, turning to tools for support with data analysis is less common than turning to leaders or PD (Marsh et al., 2006). Yet problems with current data systems and data reports undermine educators' data use:

- In a study involving interviews with education leaders in 30 school districts and charter management organizations serving approximately 2,500 to 25,000 students each, administrators reported (a) challenges in getting data out of data systems undermine data-informed instruction, and (b) it is difficult to find useful data in their systems that can be analyzed in meaningful ways (Freeland & Hernandez, 2014).

- In the same study, some school systems reported being so dissatisfied with data systems and dashboards on the market that they built their own in-house data systems (Freeland & Hernandez, 2014).

- According to Thomas Kane, a professor at Harvard Graduate School of Education and a faculty director for the Center for Education Policy Research, data analysis problems are often not related to the data not being collected; rather, they relate to the data not being organized in a way that can answer questions, which are answerable but not being asked (Davis, 2013).

- When it comes to data systems at the state level, most attention goes toward technology aspects such as hardware and software, and any reports they generate for educators do not answer questions they could already answer without the system (Data Quality Campaign, 2011).

- Score reports designed specifically for administrators are frequently not designed in ways that are easy for administrators to interpret (VanWinkle et al., 2011).

- Teachers often underutilize data systems, finding available data to be unsatisfactory or late, having a hard time locating needed data, and finding the system to be hard to use (Cho & Wayman, 2012).

- 67 percent of 4,600 surveyed teachers indicated they were not satisfied with the digital data tools they use (Bill and Melinda Gates Foundation, 2015).

- A study by the U.S. Department of Education found data systems are frequently of limited use in informing instruction because of limitations in terms of the system's data, interface, or tools (Faria et al., 2012).

There are many types of data reporting tools. It can help to consider one as an example. One of the most common types of data system, in which some data reports are commonly embedded, is the student information system (SIS). In a survey and focus group study involving 716 district, school, and technology leaders and 1,010 teachers, Gartner and the Bill and Melinda Gates Foundation (2014) found:

- **Dissatisfaction**—Only 46 percent of teachers, 35 percent of school leaders, and 47 percent of district leaders are satisfied with their SIS.

- **Limited Reporting**—Only 51 percent of teachers believe the SIS helps them monitor student progress; only 19 percent of school leaders and 11 percent of district leaders believe it supports state reporting/policies; and only 4 percent of district leaders identify simplified reporting as one of their SIS benefits.

- **Inefficient**—Only 37 percent of teachers believe their SIS aids school efficiency, and only 8 percent of district leaders identify increased efficiency as one of their SIS benefits.

- **Cumbersome**—Only 29 percent of teachers believe their SIS lets them spend more time on teaching and less on administrative tasks, and only 29 percent of teachers find it intuitive to learn to do new things on the SIS.

- **Disconnected from Instruction**—Only 23 percent of teachers believe their SIS's data helps them plan classroom activities; only 47 percent of school leaders and 25 percent of district leaders believe their SIS aids curriculum planning/policies; and only 37 percent of school leaders and 24 percent of district leaders believe their SIS supports other instructional policies.

- **Disconnection from Programs**—Only 44 percent of school leaders and 23 percent of district leaders believe their SIS is able to support program planning/policies; and only 37 percent of school leaders and 20 percent of district leaders believe their SIS supports academic program review or evaluation/policies.

- **Disconnection from Long-Term Goals**—Only 40 percent of school leaders and 22 percent of district leaders believe their SIS supports long-term strategic planning/policies.

Data Reports Are the Silent Star

- **Unsupportive of Teachers**—Only 23 percent of teachers believe they are getting the most value from the SIS's data; only 36 percent of school leaders and 26 percent of district leaders believe it supports teacher performance/policies.

- **Barriers to Use**—Teachers report the following as barriers to increased use of the SIS in the classroom: the SIS does not solve important problems in the classroom (71 percent of teachers identify this as a barrier); there is a lack of shortcuts, so users have to complete many steps for a task such as running a report (70 percent); settings and content are too "one size fits all" (66 percent); it is not easy to incorporate into the teacher's curriculum (62 percent); and teachers are unsure how to best integrate the SIS with classroom instruction (61 percent). Thirty-three percent of teachers report their SISs do not perform well in the functions most important to them; for example, only 14 percent of teachers believe the SIS performs well in generating student performance reports.

Yikes! Many educators do not ask for more than a data system that gives all educators access to data, when there is so much more their data systems could do to actively help educators make easy, good use of data. For example, one change shared in this book (arming educators with reference guides, one form of supplemental documentation) has been shown to *quadruple* educators' understanding of given data.

It Is up to You to Help

DSRPs often assume the client always knows best. This is true in many instances, but busy educators do not have time to research the best data reporting practices. In fact, the data reporting format that users report preferring can be the opposite of the report format they most accurately interpret and most appropriately use (Hattie, 2010). Educators are assuming their DSRP is doing such research. This book's author has done that research for you.

Most educators cannot or do not build their own data reports. Educators usually only control data use climate and on-site data user support. It is up to those who create education data reports—such as educator leaders and edtech vendors—to provide educators with the most effective data tools.

Over-the-Counter Data = Data that Works

The improved data tools you provide to educators with the help of this book will actively improve educators' data use, save educators' time, and reduce educators' frustration. You *can* make data reports and/or data systems that work for those who view and use them.

Over-the-Counter Data = Data that Works

If something is "over-the-counter" it is easy to access and use successfully. On this note, it would be negligent and dangerous for over-the-counter medicine to be sold without a label other than a mere heading such as "Cold" or "Flu." Rather, an over-the-counter product offers embedded guidance (e.g., a detailed label and more) explaining the product's ingredients, purpose, dangers, dosage instructions, and anything else you would need to know in order to use the contents correctly.

Educators use data to "treat" students, given the proven benefits of data. Most of them acquire this data from reports, typically generated within a data system or created by a colleague using exported data (you might even be one of those helpful colleagues). Fifty-nine percent of teachers even use data while on their own (USDEOPEPD, 2009).

Unfortunately, the data reporting tools educators use to consume data typically do not provide supports (or enough supports) to help educators understand how to use the reports' contents properly (VanWinkle et al., 2011). The previous section offered evidence of this. Educators are using data that are not presented in an "over-the-counter" format, so there are no embedded supports to ensure the data are used easily and correctly. The ramifications are rampant errors with most data analyses (covered in the section on the data analysis error epidemic earlier in this chapter).

Rather than leaving users to guess (often incorrectly) how to properly use and understand a potent tool like medicine or data, a tool that is over-the-counter offers components to actively reduce detriments and increase benefits. The pharmaceutical example in Table 1.1 helps illustrate each component's importance when it comes to how data is communicated to educators.

When these five components are added successfully to a data reporting environment, educators can easily know what the data means and how to use it. The good news is that you—as a provider of data reports, data systems, or edtech with a data/feedback component—can give this to educators.

Table 1.1

Over-the-Counter Component	You Have Seen It Look Like This in Over-the-Counter Medicine	It Can Look Like This in Data Reporting Tools
Label	The container label provides the name and information answering questions such as, "How many should I take?" and "What are the possible side effects?"	The report has a clear and concise title, and an annotation such as a footer provides the information most relevant and important to using the report's data properly.
Supplemental Documentation	Not all the information a user needs to know can fit on the label, so a folded-up piece of paper is enclosed within the package to offer further explanation.	Similarly, explanatory information specific to each report, such as a reference sheet and reference guide, can accompany each report via links and handouts.
Help System	Users want an online help system; e.g., 50 million people use WebMD every year (Kronstadt et al., 2009).	An online help system can offer comprehensive lessons on using the data system *and* on data analysis.
Package/Display	How the product is displayed and packaged helps communicate its correct purpose and use.	How data is organized and displayed, such as layout that encourages *correct* analyses for each particular report, helps to avoid confusion.
Content	The ingredients of the product are vital; they have to be effective, user-appropriate, and not expired.	The contents of each report and the report suite as a whole should be effective, audience-appropriate, and not expired.

Everyone Benefits, Including You

If you follow the lessons in this book to implement the OTCD Standards, you will likely render the following for any company or organization providing tools to educator staff:

- reduced workload for Customer Support (e.g., fewer complaints, requests, and misunderstandings);
- reduced workload for programmers and everyone involved in product development (e.g., reduced client requests and needs for revisions);
- a more effective product (e.g., easier, increased sales).

Best of all, this book will make it easy for you to improve your data systems/reports so they actively improve data use, save educators' time, and reduce educators' frustration. Essentially, this book will help you make data reports that work for those who view and use them.

Notes

1 *The Wall Street Journal* reflects this book's use of "data *is*" and "data *are*": "Most style guides and dictionaries have come to accept the use of the noun data with either singular or plural verbs, and we hereby join the majority" (Izzo, 2012, p. 1).

2 The average IQ of a college graduate is 121+ and of most Ph.D. recipients is 132+ (Hurley, 2012), whereas the average IQ of the general population is considered 100 (Weiss, 2009); since only 30.4 percent of the general population of an age comparable to teachers holds a college degree (Pérez-Peña, 2012), whereas nearly all educators are college graduates (at a minimum), educators' IQs are likely to be above those of the general population as a whole.

References

American Institutes for Research (AIR) (2013). *Most teachers "highly qualified" under NCLB standards, but teacher qualifications lag in many high poverty and high minority schools.* Retrieved from www.air.org/reports-products/index.cfm?fa= viewContent&content_id=417 (accessed October 30, 2015).

Bill and Melinda Gates Foundation (2012). *Innovation in education: Technology and effective teaching in the U.S.* Retrieved from https://edsurge.s3.amazon aws.com/public/BMGF_Innovation_In_Education.pdf (assessed May 21, 2003).

Bill and Melinda Gates Foundation (2014). *Primary sources: America's teachers on teaching in an era of change: A project of Scholastic and the Bill and Melinda Gates Foundation (3rd ed.).* Retrieved from www.scholastic.com/primarysources/ download-the-full-report.htm (accessed October 30, 2015).

Bill and Melinda Gates Foundation (2015). *Teachers know best: Making data work for teachers and students.* Retrieved from https://s3.amazonaws.com/edtech-production/reports/Gates-TeachersKnowBest-MakingDataWork.pdf (accessed October 30, 2015).

Cho, V., & Wayman, J. C. (2012). Districts' efforts for data use and computer data systems: The role of sensemaking in system use and implementation. *2012 Annual Meeting of the American Educational Research Association, Vancouver, British Columbia, Canada.* Retrieved from www.vincentcho.com/uploads/9/6/5/2/ 9652180/cho_wayman_aera_2012_final.pdf (accessed October 30, 2015).

Data Quality Campaign (2011). *Leveraging the power of state longitudinal data systems: Building capacity to turn data into useful information.* Retrieved from www.dataqualitycampaign.org/wp-content/uploads/files/1303_DQC-Research %20capacity%20May17.pdf (accessed October 30, 2015).

Davis, M. R. (2013, October 1). Managing the digital district: Intelligent data analysis helps predict needs. *Education Week,* 33(6), 20–21. Bethesda, MD: Editorial Projects in Education.

Faria, A., Heppen, J., Li, Y., Stachel, S., Jones, W., Sawyer, K., Palacios, M. et al. (2012, Summer). *Charting success: Data use and student achievement in urban schools.* Council of the Great City Schools and the American Institutes for Research. Retrieved from www.cgcs.org/cms/lib/DC00001581/Centricity/ Domain/87/Charting_Success.pdf (accessed October 30, 2015).

Freeland, J., & Hernandez, A. (2014, June). *Schools and software: What's now and what's next.* San Mateo, CA: Clayton Christensen Institute for Disruptive Innovation. Retrieved from www.christenseninstitute.org/publications/schools-and-software/ (accessed October 30, 2015).

Gartner and the Bill and Melinda Gates Foundation (2014). *Closing the gap: turning SIS/LMS data into action: Report: Education community attitudes toward SIS/LMS solutions.* Retrieved from www.cosn.org/sites/default/files/implementation_and_ selection_approaches_toward_sis_lms_solutions.pdf (accessed October 30, 2015).

Hattie, J. (2010). Visibly learning from reports: The validity of score reports. *Online Educational Research Journal.* Retrieved from www.oerj.org/View?action= viewPaper&paper=6 (accessed October 30, 2015).

Hurley, D. (2012, April 22). Can you build a (better brain?). *The New York Times,* MM38.

Izzo, P. (2012, July 5). Is data is, or is data ain't, a plural? *The Wall Street Journal*. Retrieved from http://blogs.wsj.com/economics/2012/07/05/is-data-is-or-is-data-aint-a-plural/ (accessed October 30, 2015).

Kidron, Y. (2012, April). Strategies click into place: Online resources translate research to practice. *JSD: The Learning Forward Journal*, 33(2), 44–47. Oxford, OH: Learning Forward.

Killion, J., & Hirsh, S. (2012, February). The bottom line on excellence: A guide to investing in professional learning that increases educator performance and student results. *JSD: The Learning Forward Journal*, 33(1), 10–16. Oxford, OH: Learning Forward.

Kronstadt, J., Moiduddin, A., & Sellheim, W. (2009, March). *Consumer use of computerized applications to address health and health care needs: Prepared for U.S. Department of Health and Human Services, Office of the Secretary, Assistant Secretary for Planning and Evaluation*. Bethesda, MD: NORC at the University of Chicago.

McDonald, S., Andal, J., Brown, K., & Schneider, B. (2007). *Getting the evidence for evidence-based initiatives: How the Midwest states use data systems to improve education processes and outcomes (Issues & Answers Report, REL 2007–No. 016)*. Washington, DC: U.S. Department of Education, Institute of Education Sciences, National Center for Education Evaluation and Assistance, Regional Educational Laboratory Midwest.

Marsh, J. A., Pane, J. F., & Hamilton, L. S. (2006). *Making sense of data-driven decision making in education: Evidence from recent RAND research*. Santa Monica, CA: RAND Corporation.

Northwest Evaluation Association (NWEA) (2014). *Make assessment matter: Students and educators want tests that support learning*. Portland, OR: Author. [Also retrieved from https://legacysupport.nwea.org/sites/www.nwea.org/files/resources/MakeAssessmentMatter_5-2014.pdf (accessed October 30, 2015)]

Papay, J., Harvard Graduate School of Education (2007). *Aspen Institute datasheet: The teaching workforce*. Washington, DC: The Aspen Institute.

Pérez-Peña, R. (2012, February 24). Milestone is passed as 30 percent of U.S. adults report having a college degree. *The New York Times*, A17. New York, NY: New York Times Company Inc.

Rankin, J. G. (2013). *Over-the-counter data's impact on educators' data analysis accuracy*. ProQuest Dissertations and Theses, 3575082. Retrieved from http://pqdtopen.proquest.com/doc/1459258514.html?FMT=ABS (accessed October 30, 2015).

Sparks, S. D. (2014, July 25). Can states make student data useful for schools? *Education Week*. Retrieved from http://blogs.edweek.org/edweek/inside-school-research/2014/07/can_states_turn_slag_data_into.html (accessed October 30, 2015).

Underwood, J. S., Zapata-Rivera, D., & VanWinkle, W. (2008) Growing pains: Teachers using and learning to use IDMS. *ETS Research Memorandum RM-08-07*. Princeton, NJ: ETS.

U.S. Department of Education Office of Educational Technology (2012). *Enhancing teaching and learning through educational data mining and learning analytics: An issue brief*. Washington, DC: Author.

U.S. Department of Education Office of Planning, Evaluation and Policy Development (2009). *Implementing data-informed decision making in schools: Teacher access, supports and use*. United States Department of Education (ERIC Document Reproduction Service No. ED504191).

U.S. Department of Education Office of Planning, Evaluation and Policy Development (2011). *Teachers' ability to use data to inform instruction: Challenges and supports*. United States Department of Education (ERIC Document Reproduction Service No. ED516494).

Van der Meij, H. (2008). Designing for user cognition and affect in a manual. Should there be special support for the latter? *Learning and Instruction*, 18(1), 18–29.

VanWinkle, W., Vezzu, M., & Zapata-Rivera, D. (2011). Question-based reports for policymakers. *ETS Research Memorandum RM-11-16*. Princeton, NJ: ETS.

Wayman, J. C., Cho, V., & Johnston, M. T. (2007). *The data-informed district: A district-wide evaluation of data use in the Natrona County School District*. Austin, TX: The University of Texas.

Weiss, V. (2009). National IQ means transformed from Programme for International Student Assessment (PISA) scores, and their underlying gene frequencies. *The Journal of Social, Political and Economic Studies*, 34(1), 71–94. Munich, Germany: German Central Office for Genealogy.

Zapata-Rivera, D., & VanWinkle, W. (2010). A research-based approach to designing and evaluating score reports for teachers. *ETS Research Memorandum RM-10-01*. Princeton, NJ: ETS.

2 Label Standards

Definition of Label

A label is text on each data report and on each data report list that helps educators better understand the report's content. Data that is "over-the-counter" is reported with two types of label:

- an effective report **title** (sometimes called a header), which is the text at the top of the report;
- an effective **footer** (or other annotation), which is text located directly on the data report (e.g., the bottom of the page if printed, and the bottom of the screen or image if viewed on a computer screen).

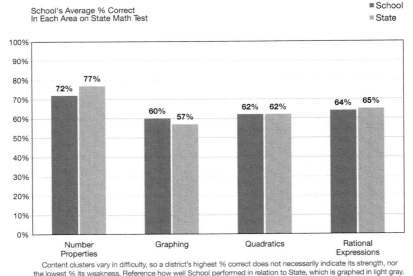

Figure 2.1

The purpose of the title and footer is to help the user easily understand and use the data.

You would not expect an educator to consume over-the-counter medicine from a bottle that read "Flu" and nothing else: no more in the title to indicate if it is for a cold flu vs. stomach flu, and no label outlining ingredients, symptoms treated, how many pills to take, or dangers to consider. Taking medicine from an unmarked or marginally marked container would be negligent and dangerous. Data also impacts lives, so you should not expect an educator to consume data from data reports featuring poor titles (e.g., test title) and/or no footers or helpful annotations. Educators use data reports to make decisions that impact kids, so they should be given adequate labeling to support their use of these high stakes tools.

How to Implement Label Standards

Resources

Access the following:

- OTCD *Label* standards (on pages 1–2 of OTCD Standards)
- Details on research-based evidence supporting OTCD *Label* standards

An ideal data reporting environment should reflect the OTCD *Label* standards, which stipulate research-based ways data systems/ reports can provide titles and footers. These standards can be found online with details on the extensive research informing every standard. The rest of this chapter contains a lesson on how to implement each OTCD *Label* standard.

Real-World Implementation: Label (Footers)

By Lane D. Rankin, CEO/Founder, Illuminate Education

When Dr. Jenny Rankin and I first met she kept talking about footers. I was still running DataDirector at the time, having recently sold the company to Harcourt, and she explained how much more educators would understand the data if footers were present on data reports. The evidence supporting footers was very compelling. When I left DataDirector and founded Illuminate Education a year later, I vowed every report we built would contain a footer.

Standard 1.2.01: Present

The best part about implementing footers for all our reports is how easy it has been, from a technical standpoint. Once your report expert (an educator who deeply understands how educators will use each report) writes the footer, all the programmer has to do is paste it into place. We even made some of our footers dynamic, displaying guidance catered to the way users run the report via input control selection.

Standard 1.2.02: Only Communicate Most Crucial Info

When you train educators on how to use a data report, there is usually one piece of information you most need to tell them. The footer is the perfect place for this information. Feedback from data coaches and administrators has been that footers support them in their efforts to improve site- and district-wide data use. Feedback from users of all educator roles has been that footers make their jobs easier and prevent them from making mistakes.

Standard 1.2.03: Follow Length Guidelines (Short)

We use footer length guidelines in keeping with the Rankin (2013) study: 328 characters max for horizontal reports, and 243 characters max for vertical reports. There are some rare exceptions, but keeping to these limits for most reports means users are likely to read the footers. Otherwise the footers will not help them, and helping stakeholders is our most important job.

Standard 1.2.04: Follow Font Guidelines (Same Size/Type as Report's Data)

To best help educators and their students, the report footers cannot be easy to miss. Matching the footer's font and size to the rest of the report helps users treat the footer as being as important as the data itself.

We are in the business of education data to help educators do their jobs while making their lives easier. Footers assist us in accomplishing this goal. We are partners in helping educators help kids, and this means we have a moral responsibility to give users data in a way that benefits kids (not hurts kids, which poorly presented data can do when it misinforms). If the purpose of a data display is to communicate data, it needs a footer as one of many means to ensure understanding.

Titles

Standard 1.1.01: Present

Give each report its own, distinct title, which remains consistent between (a) when it is displayed within a report list and (b) when it is featured directly on the report, in which case it should be prominent at the top of the page.

When viewing reports, teachers indicate wanting clearer titles (Hattie, 2010). This need extends to stakeholders in non-teaching roles, as well. All reports should be clearly titled and labeled so all stakeholders (including educators and non-educators) can easily understand the data (James-Ward et al., 2013).

Label Standards

> ## *Sample Report List Excerpt*
>
> 1-to-1 Correlation
>
> 1-to-1 Correlation Growth
>
> Content Area Focus
>
> Content Area Growth
>
> Etc.

Report List

A "report list" is a place (often within a page or module in a data system or other edtech product) where users can view all of the report offerings at once, albeit with possible page breaks. Having such a list is vital to the data investigation process, where educators must be able to search and skim report titles to locate those best suited to their needs. Each report on this list should have its own, distinct title, which matches the title featured on the actual report.

Report

Each report should have a title (matching that on the report list) displayed prominently at the top of the report. This means at the top of the screen (when the report is being viewed online, such as within a data system) and at the top of the page (when the report has been printed). A slightly larger font size in bold will help distinguish the title from other text on the page and offer immediate recognition of the report's nature. This can be seen in the report examples shown in the "Package/Display Standards: Report Design" chapter.

Label Standards

Standard 1.1.02: Communicate What Is Inside the Report

Clearly communicate what type of data the report displays and/or how it displays data (e.g., report type). Use a title that functions well both (a) when the report is closed and users are determining which report(s) to open/view in the data system, and (b) when the report is open (viewed within the data system or printed) and users need a quick indication of its contents.

Just as a medication label bears the title of its contents, a report title should appropriately communicate what type of data the report displays and/or how it displays it (e.g., report type). However, a report title must do "double duty" in that it must function well within the report list *and* within the actual report.

Report List (When the Report Is Closed or Not yet Present)

When educators are determining which report(s) to access and view, they are typically viewing a list of all available report titles. This list might be within a data system, or housed on a district's staff portal, or printed for educators like a table of contents.

Even if this list features thumbnail images of the reports, it is impossible for all educators of varying vision to quickly grasp a report's contents from a small image. The report title should do a good job of communicating what type of data and/or report the educator will see if he or she clicks a particular report title/link or otherwise acquires a report. See the examples on the next two pages.

Those titles might be sufficient if educators were viewing the actual reports, but imagine how the reports would function on a report list, where educators do not have the advantage of clearly seeing what the reports look like:

- Student Score Report
- Student Performance Report

Either title could refer to either report, as neither title gives users any indication of *how* the data (which, at least one of the titles tells us, will be scores) will be reported.

19

Label Standards

Example: Imagine you titled the report below *Student Score Report* and the report on the next page *Student Performance Report*:

Student Score Report
% Correct by Standard on ELA Benchmark 10-8

Students 32 names	Grade Level	LA.8.RW.1.3 3Qs = 8% of test	LA.8.RC.2.2 7Qs = 18% of test	LA.8.RC.2.7 5Qs = 13% of test	LA.8.RL.3.2 2Qs = 5% of test	LA.8.RL.3.6 3Qs = 8% of test	LA.8.WC.1.3 4Qs = 10% of test	LA.8.WC.1.4 8Qs = 20% of test	LA.8.WS.1.1 5Qs = 13% of test	LA.8.WS.1.3 3Qs = 8% of test
All Students	10-11	77	79	83	72	86	82	75	79	70
Anduwell, Ike	10	47	100	77	100	100	82	75	100	100
Erner, Bea	10	67	71	60	87	100	75	98	100	78
Learn, Wanda	10	78	86	100	50	100	68	54	60	50
Lerner, Earl E.	10	100	50	75	76	67	75	87	87	98
Onlearner, Hans	11	82	75	98	100	89	98	94	50	65
Perbrite, Sue	10	75	98	100	78	67	100	97	76	68
Reed, Khan	10	68	54	99	50	67	99	85	100	68
Seas, Alotta	10	75	87	45	98	100	45	57	78	43
Tagraduate, Luke N.	11	98	94	73	65	100	73	72	50	50
Taker, Tess	10	100	97	67	68	67	67	71	98	87
Trihard, Will	10	99	85	100	68	67	78	86	65	50
Turner, Paige	10	45	57	90	43	100	100	50	68	76
Wright, Mark	10	73	72	100	50	100	100	47	100	77

Figure 2.2

Label Standards

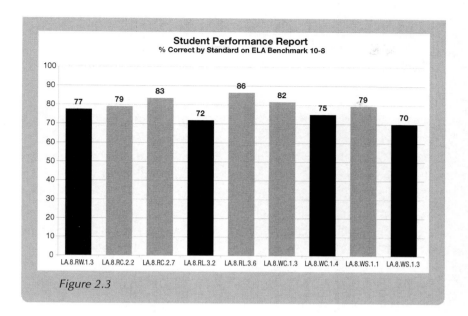

Figure 2.3

Now imagine changing the report titles by keeping "Student Score" (an indication of the type of data reported) but replacing the word "report" with "list" or "summary" to better suggest *how* the data will be presented:

- Student Score List
- Student Performance Summary

See how "list" better suggests opening the report will lead to a list format, as seen in the first of the two report excerpts shown. Also see how "summary" better suggests opening the report will lead to something like the second of the two report excerpts shown, which summarizes all of the students' scores.

If each report utilizes a wide variety of display formats (list, summary, distribution, breakdown, seating charts, etc.), you can forgo these indicators in the titles and instead communicate the formats through the:

- **report list** (where a matrix format can display an "X" under each format used); this is further explained for Standard 5.2.04 in the "Content Standards" chapter;

Label Standards

- **filters** that can lead users to reports that include the format(s) selected; this is further explained for Standard 4.5.01 in the "Package/Display Standards: User Interface" chapter.

Report (When the Report Is Open or Present)

Once a report is being viewed (either within the data system or printed and viewed elsewhere), the report title should still do a good job of communicating what type of data the educator is looking at. It should be featured prominently at the top of the page (this is sometimes called the page header). Multiple reports are often printed and distributed/viewed as a set, so the user should be able to easily distinguish between the reports by merely looking at the titles.

Key ancillary information—such as the type of data the user selected (using input controls) for the report to display—should be displayed clearly under the report title (see Figure 2.4). However, this supplemental information should be displayed less prominently than the title. This allows the title to remain easy to distinguish quickly.

Consistency

The same title should be used when the report is closed and when it is open. In other words, it should not change. The ancillary information, which is dependent upon within-report input controls and thus varies, should not be displayed in the report list. Ancillary information should only show on the report itself. If the following information was displayed at the top of a report, the top line would be the report title, and the bottom line would be the ancillary information:

> Student Score Report
> % Correct by Standard on ELA Benchmark 10–8

A list of static reports (such as provided by an educator leader on a staff portal) can be an exception to the above rule if the ancillary information is easily distinguishable from the titles. For example, a table might be

22

used to list report titles in the first column, with the permanent ancillary information in the second column.

Standard 1.1.03: Use Consistent Titling System

Utilize a consistent titling system within the data system or report suite. For example, if one report title ends with the word "List" to indicate that its format involves listing scores of multiple entities, titles of like reports should also end with "List."

A collection of reports should utilize a highly consistent titling system. For example, any time multiple entities are *listed* on a report (e.g., a list of teachers with their data, where each row belongs to a single teacher and contains averages of his or her students' scores on a test), a report collection might refer to that type of report as a list and include the word "list" in the report's title.

Whatever naming conventions you choose to use, consistency will make it easier for users to:

- know what to look for when users are searching for a particular type of report;
- find reports, such as by skimming the report list and/or using filters to narrow down the report list;
- understand what a report will look like (and thus if it is vs. is not what users are looking for) without having to open it first;
- feel an increasing sense of ease in the report environment's use, as users' knowledge of reports they *have* used will transfer better to understanding the nature of reports they have *not yet* used when the titles are similar and consistent.

Including variety that does not have meaning is a common problem with the design of reporting environments such as dashboards (Few, 2006). The concept of consistency is developed further in the "Design Consistency" section of the "Package/Display Standards: User Interface" chapter of this book.

23

Label Standards

Standard 1.1.04: Use Concise Language that Maximizes Info Communicated

Be concise while also communicating the most pertinent info a user needs to know when determining if this is the report he or she needs; i.e., do not try to accommodate all of a report's descriptors in its title. Be as concise as good sense allows; e.g., the term "3-Yr" works better than "Multi-Yr" in the title of a report that displays up to three years of data because "3-Yr" communicates more info while also using fewer characters (reducing clutter).

Data reports should avoid trying to communicate too much information, which is a common mistake (Underwood, 2013). One area in which an overabundance of information can appear is the title.

Too much text can overwhelm users and increase the words' chances of being ignored entirely (Hattie, 2010; Zapata-Rivera & VanWinkle, 2010). It would be ill-advised to try to accommodate all of a report's descriptors in its title, but there are many instances in which a title can provide educators with a better understanding of the report's contents before the user even opens the report.

The trick for titles is being as concise as good sense allows while also communicating as much of the *most pertinent* information a user needs to know when determining if this is the report he or she needs to view.

Example: Instead of using "Multi-Yr" in the title of a report that allows up to three years of data to be displayed, it is better to use "3-Yr" because it is shorter and more descriptive. Using four characters instead of eight (that is, half as many characters), "3-Yr" adds less clutter to the title while simultaneously communicating more. Even if a district has only added two years of data to the system generating this report, so that the report only displays two years of data, users would know not to waste time searching for a different report if they wanted three years of data, as this was the right report. They could then spend that time contacting a system administrator to request that an additional year's data be added.

24

Avoid Questions

It is far less concise to title a report "How are my students performing?" (27 characters) than "Student Score List" (16 characters; nearly half as many), even though the latter communicates far more about what is reported (student scores) and how it is reported (as a list). The initial words in questions ("How are . . . ", "Where is . . . ", "Why are . . . ", etc.) add unnecessary clutter to titles, as does the question mark at the end.

In addition, a question is typically a complete sentence which thus requires a verb, which must be communicated in a single tense (e.g., performed, perform/performs, performing, will perform). Since a single report can typically be generated with different years' data and for different roster years (e.g., last year's test scores of incoming students, last year's test scores of last year's students, test scores students acquired after promotion to the next grade, etc.), using a single verb tense can imply a report will not suit an educator's needs when it actually will.

Likewise, the number of questions educators could ask (and use a single report to answer) is virtually infinite, which means a question-based title does not work well for an education data report. This concept is developed further in the "Content Standards" chapter for Standard 5.2.03. However, peeking at "Sample Questions Data Can Help Answer" provides a sample of the infinite questions in education data investigations. It would be a bonus for a data system to allow a question- or theory-based search to render a report generated in a way that specifically addresses the question or theory that was posed. However, an individual report should not be built for (and thus not titled to match) single questions.

Favor Nouns and Modifiers

Consider how much stronger these titles become when non-nouns and redundant nouns are removed:

- **Removing Preposition, Adverb, and Verb**—"List of How Subgroups Scored" (24 characters) becomes "Subgroup Score List" (17 characters).
- **Removing Article and Redundant Nouns** "The Subgroup Score List Report" (26 characters) becomes "Subgroup Score List" (17 characters).

Determine which words in your report titles need to be removed, rearranged, shortened, or replaced. As you make these changes, remember the previous standards covered so titles maximize consistency and value. Also read the "Content Standards" chapter, which further informs report titles and shares other options for supporting question-driven data investigation.

Standard 1.1.05: Leave Some Info for the Header and/or Input Controls

Do not cram ancillary info (that can be determined by users' input control selections) into the title. Instead, let users control details such as "Students: Asian," "Grouped by: Course," etc. and display these selections *under* the report's title in a less prominent font.

A recurring theme in good data system and report design is *avoid clutter*. Clutter leaves users less likely to find what they need, less likely to use the system again, and more likely to feel frustrated. Most importantly, this leaves them less likely to be able to use the data system or report suite to help students.

Uncluttered Titles

Titles should thus be concise. Consider which words in a prospective title would function better elsewhere in the report page's header, as determined by users' input control selections. In other words, when the report is displayed on the screen or printed, ancillary information can appear underneath the report title. Examples of this secondary information include the administration date of the test for which data is being

Example: Consider a long title like this:

English II (Course #00455) Teacher List at Ames High 2011–2012 Students in Grade 10 Performance on 2011–2012 English Lang. Arts CST Test

displayed or the enrollment year of the students whose scores are being displayed.

Yikes—that title is 116 characters long. Not only would such a title add clutter to the top of the report, but a report list consisting of titles this long and convoluted would be exceptionally slow to navigate. In addition, these more specific titles limit what each report is designed to do, thus requiring more reports to be made. An unnecessarily long report list makes it even harder for educators to find the specific reports they need.

If we reduce the report's title to just three of its words—Teacher Performance List (22 characters)—we can move the ancillary information to below the title. A less prominent font (e.g., smaller and not bold) than the title is used for ancillary information so the two information types do not compete for attention.

In Figure 2.4 notice how much easier it is to locate key information (e.g., students' enrollment year), which will make it easier for educators to compare reports and distinguish differences.

Uncluttered Report List

Implementing this standard also results in a less cluttered report list. A common example of cluttering report titles (and thus report lists) with information that could be relegated to ancillary information occurs in test-based titles. See the example on page 29.

The way the reports were set up in the data system, with a different report title (and thus a different report on the report list) for each STAR test, educators had to go through the following whenever they were viewing the results of one test type (e.g., CST) and wanted to switch to another test type (e.g., CMA):

1. Go back to the report search/list (see Figure 2.5).

2. Find the "new" report (e.g., find *CMA Scores Student List* as opposed to *CST Scores Student List*), possibly using filters and search words to find it.

3. Open the new report, likely losing (and thus having to reenter) any input control selections already made (e.g., only wanting the report to include results for socioeconomically disadvantaged students).

Multiple Entities' Measure Comparison List

Assessment: 2/20/14, ELA Benchmark 7

Course: Ames High, English II (00455)

Students: Accountability Subgroups, Local Data, 2012–2013 Grade 10

Accountability Subgroups	# of Students	Performance Level Distribution						% of students scoring within each level	Performance Level			Performance Level	
		Far Below Basic	Below Basic	Basic	Proficient	Advanced	Prof & Advanced		Performance Level	Gap			Gap
All Students	491	5 / 27	7 / 33	16 / 81	42 / 208	29 / 142	71 / 350	5 7 16% 42% 29%	3.6	0.0			0.0
Af.Amer./Black	97	0 / 0	5 / 5	19 / 18	33 / 32	43 / 42	76 / 74	5 19 33% 43%	3.8	0.3			0.3
Amer. Indian/AN	90	0 / 0	2 / 2	13 / 12	47 / 42	38 / 34	84 / 76	13% 47% 38%	4.2	0.7			0.7
Asian	45	7 / 3	7 / 3	29 / 13	38 / 17	20 / 9	58 / 26	7 7 29% 38% 20%	2.9	-0.7	-0.7		
Filipino	102	12 / 12	2 / 2	17 / 17	53 / 54	17 / 17	70 / 71	12 17% 53% 17%	3.5	-0.1	-0.1		
Hispanic/Latino	46	7 / 3	17 / 8	26 / 12	39 / 18	11 / 5	50 / 23	7 17% 26% 39% 11	2.5	-1.1	-1.1		
NH/Pac.Islander	70	1 / 1	4 / 3	6 / 4	61 / 43	27 / 19	89 / 62	4 6 61% 27%	4.4	0.9			0.9
White	41	20 / 8	24 / 10	12 / 5	5 / 2	39 / 16	44 / 18	20% 24% 12 5 39%	2.2	-1.4	-1.4		
2 or More Races	12	8 / 1	0 / 0	0 / 0	17 / 2	75 / 9	92 / 11	8 17% 75%	4.6	1.0			1.0
Socioec.Disadv.	32	6 / 2	22 / 7	22 / 7	31 / 10	19 / 6	50 / 16	6 22% 22% 31% 19%	2.5	-1.1	-1.1		
English Learner	60	7 / 4	30 / 18	13 / 8	43 / 26	7 / 4	50 / 30	7 30% 13% 43% 7	2.5	-1.1	-1.1		
Students with Disab.	27	15 / 4	44 / 12	15 / 4	15 / 4	11 / 3	26 / 7	15% 44% 15% 15% 11	1.3	-2.3	-2.3		

Find the largest red bars on the right-hand graph (showing gaps between a subgroup's students and those not in the subgroup) to spot likely achievement gaps.

Figure 2.4

Some of a Data System's Report Titles

CAPA Scores Site List
CAPA Scores Student List
CAPA Scores Student List by Course
CAPA Scores Teacher List
CAPA Scores Teacher List by Course
CMA Scores Site List
CMA Scores Student List
CMA Scores Student List by Course
CMA Scores Teacher List
CMA Scores Teacher List by Course
CST Scores Site List
CST Scores Student List
CST Scores Student List by Course
CST Scores Teacher List
CST Scores Teacher List by Course
STS Scores Site List
STS Scores Student List
STS Scores Student List by Course
STS Scores Teacher List
STS Scores Teacher List by Course

Example: The long list above represents some of the report titles offered on a data system's report list. In the state where this report list is used, "STAR testing" took place, and CAPA, CMA, CST, and STS (i.e., the data types listed here) were all examples of a single state testing program known as STAR. They were similar in structure and in terms of how their data was reported, with the CAPA being the most dissimilar. Since students took different STAR tests based on English Learner (EL) and Special Education statuses, educators viewing their students' data often needed to switch back and forth between test results to get a complete picture of their students' performance.

Label Standards

As a solution, these reports could be consolidated into "STAR" reports (as STAR was the testing program to which each test in the example belonged). Input controls could then allow users to easily switch back and

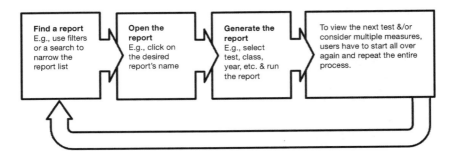

Figure 2.5 Problem with Using Ancillary Info-Specific Data Reports

forth between specific tests. The reports could still be separate reports "behind the scenes" (e.g., to make design variations based on user selections easier to manage, and to speed up how quickly the data system could display the report since more input controls can otherwise mean longer generation time if they are kept within a single report). However, in the user's eyes they would all seem to function as one report.

Consolidated Report Titles

STAR Scores Site List

STAR Scores Student List

STAR Scores Teacher List

Also, there were separate reports titled "by Course". That setup:

- clutters the report titles on which it is featured;
- clutters the report list by making it unnecessarily longer;

Label Standards

- forces users into time-consuming steps (shown in Figure 2.5) when they open a report and run it, only to find out it's not the exact format they were looking for and thus they have to return to the report list to find another, slightly different report.

Thus these "by Course" reports should be removed and "by course" should be a variation allowed by the main report's input controls (and mentioned underneath the title on the report, along with other ancillary information).

By simply following the two recommendations discussed above, the twenty reports listed above are now consolidated into just three reports (shown on the previous page). Input controls allow for variations without losing any of the options.

The twenty reports originally listed comprised a single segment of the data system's report list. In a list of fifty or more reports, it is immensely difficult for users (particular new users or users easily intimidated by data or technology) to find the report(s) they need. Your report list should be as short as possible, while remaining descriptive, so users:

- can easily find the report(s) they need;

- do not waste time unnecessarily wading through a long list;

- do not become frustrated and/or give up on using the data system;

- (due to the bullets above, and most importantly) are better able to use data to help students.

As an optional step, depending on how overtaxed your input controls are, the report list types (e.g., site, student, or teacher) could also be handled by input controls to turn the original example of twenty reports into a single report without losing any report options. Even if only *some* report consolidation opportunities are taken, it will likely be an improvement.

However, keeping reports test-specific is still not ideal. Please see the Standard 4.4.03 and "Input Controls" sections of the "Package/Display Standards: User Interface" chapter for more for details on how additional changes can render reports better suited for data investigation. For example, steering away from test-specific titles better supports the use of multiple measures and recommended data investigation practices.

Label Standards

If Your Reports Are Not Dynamic

Some of you reading this book provide educators with static reports you build for them outside of a data system. Your report users thus do not have the option of making input control selections. If this is the case, consider how many reports you offer users (i.e., how many reports are listed in the report list from which users select reports to view). If your list contains twenty or more reports, it can be helpful to group and categorize them wherever they are listed for users. For example, you could indicate which five particular reports are all Performance Growth reports, which six particular reports are all Class Roster lists, etc.

Footers

Standard 1.2.01: Present

Place a report-specific footer (as described in this section) on each data report.

An effective footer (or other annotation) offering report-specific data analysis guidance should be displayed directly on each data report. The term *footer* is used in OTCD Standards rather than *annotation* simply because *footer* is more descriptive of where most report annotations tend to appear. Annotations elsewhere in the report, however, are also effective. Complex reports with multiple data displays can feature multiple annotations to help educators understand and use the report's data.

A quantitative study (Rankin, 2013) presented 211 educators (of varied backgrounds and roles at nine elementary and secondary schools) with graphical and tabular reports, which these educators then used to answer multiple data analysis questions. Each data report set looked the same and contained the same data from assessments participants likely worked with regularly, yet the report sets differed in terms of whether or not they offered added textual guidance to help users analyze the reports' contents. Significant findings:

- Educators whose data reports featured footers (which offered analysis guidance specific to those reports) used the footers 73 percent of the time.

32

- In terms of relative and absolute differences, educators' analyses of data were 307 percent more accurate (with a 23 percentage point difference) when a footer was present and 336 percent more accurate (with a 26 percentage point difference) when respondents specifically indicated having used the footers.

The reason footers are so necessary and effective relates to education data's complex nature:

Example: Consider the graph below, which is a common format seen in data system reports. The left bar of each pairing on the graph represents a single school and charts the average percent of questions its students answered correctly within four areas known as content clusters or domains.

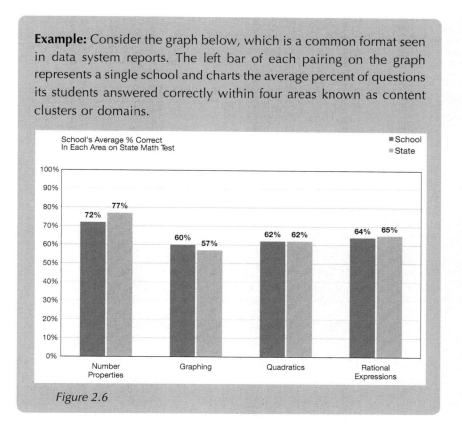

Figure 2.6

While this test is for one particular state's math proficiency test, the reporting style is common for other assessments, as well. Most people would assume educators could easily understand such a report and use the data it contains to make decisions. So, take a look at the graph and answer this question:

> Which area (e.g., *Number Properties, Graphing,* etc.) is most likely to be the school's weakness?

This is not a trick question concerning multiple measures, as you *can* determine what is—according to this report—most likely to be the school's weakness. It is safe to assume you know the importance of using multiple measures and thus you would use this report to determine a possible weakness, which you could then consider along with other measures, as well.

So, what is your answer to the above question? Considering this report, most educators would identify *Graphing* as a possible school weakness because it has the school's lowest percent correct. However, *Graphing* was actually the cluster in which the school performed *best.*

As it happens, content clusters on this particular test differ in difficulty, much like your classes differed in difficulty when you were in high school (e.g., a parent might be more pleased with your "B" in *Honors Physics* than with your "B" in *Introduction to Physical Education*: the same grade but different implications). Thus the school's highest percent correct for a cluster does not necessarily indicate its strength, and its lowest percent is not necessarily its weakness.

The state that designed this test recommends comparing the School percent to the State percent (i.e., the degree to which the school beat the scores of minimally proficient students statewide), since State performance provides us with a picture of which areas were harder for students and which were easier. In other words, you could use this formula:

School % – State % = #

The cluster with the highest difference (highest # using the above formula) could be a school strength, and the cluster with the lowest difference (lowest # using the above formula) could be a school weakness. Using this formula, *Number Properties* was the cluster in which School lagged the most behind State.

Given this added information, most educators have a completely new sense of what the data means. If they had proceeded without this information and assumed the data was simple enough to understand without it, 89 percent of educators' conclusions would have been wrong (Rankin, 2013) . . . and those faulty conclusions would have shaped actions that would impact students. Even multiple measures offer little help if their implications are misunderstood, as well. Labels such as titles and footers offer the chance to embed important analysis guidance *directly within* data reports where it is hard for educators to overlook them.

If *all* educators have time to read *all* the technical reports, post-test guides, and research reports for *all* of their datasets (many of these ranging from 150–600 pages), they might not need annotations such as footers or other textual support on their data reports. If you consider how busy educators are, you will understand educators do not have time to read and memorize everything that will help them analyze each dataset. For example, half of teachers and principals alike report they are regularly under great stress (Metropolitan Life Insurance Company, 2013).

Footers written by education data experts can alert users to possible missteps and help them avoid analysis errors most common for the particular data being viewed. Consider the graph example provided earlier in this chapter. Now, imagine the potential of a footer at the bottom of that particular report stating:

- Content clusters vary in difficulty, so a district's highest percent correct does not necessarily indicate its strength, or the lowest percent its weakness. Reference how well School performed in relation to State, which is graphed in purple.

This footer could even provide an example:

- E.g., School's score of 60 percent minus State's score of 57 percent = +3 (School did well in *Graphing*), whereas School's score of 72 percent minus State's score of 77 percent = –5 (School did more poorly in *Number Properties*).

The concept explained in this footer can be difficult to grasp, but imagine how much *more* complicated it would be if the report did not contain this textual guidance at all. Likewise, the design of this sample report (the way in which results are graphed) is highly flawed and not carrying its weight in assisting good analysis (something covered later in the "Package/Display Standards: Report Design" chapter). However, it is the most common way in which this particular data is graphed.

Many data systems market within multiple states, and while they change labels and which reports they choose to display for users, they often

Label Standards

do not devote the necessary time to customizing report formats to best suit educators' analyses. The data report example just provided, while not ideal, is nonetheless very typical. While this is a problem that should ideally be remedied (also addressed in "Package/Display Standards: Report Design"), imagine how much more important the easy inclusion and customization of footers becomes when a report's format is misleading.

The footers used in the Rankin (2013) study followed OTCD Standards covered in this book. Thus, if your data system provider implements the standards with fidelity, you can expect results similar to a 307–336 percent increase in educator colleagues' data analysis accuracy when using those reports.

You might be tempted to provide information only within other reporting tools (e.g., within the reference sheets, reference guides, and help system), and not within the actual report (e.g., within a footer). However, while many users will benefit from the supplemental documentation and help system (and thus they are important components to making data reports and data systems work), many users will never take the time or effort to find and use such ancillary resources. For example, a study of reporting practices in thirty U.S. states found explanations set apart from data displays (e.g., in an introduction or appendix) are sometimes overlooked by users; thus the most vital text must be featured in close proximity (ideally right next) to the data displays (Aschbacher & Herman, 1991).

There are certain pieces of information you will need to include in the footer in order to best help the analyses of those using the reports. Thus, a footer should be present on each report. Footers' likelihood of improving educators' data analyses by 307–336 percent makes footers a key component to making data reports work for educators.

Standard 1.2.02: Only Communicate Most Crucial Info

Only include info that is crucial for users to correctly understand and interpret the data. For example, clearly communicate how users can avoid the mistakes or confusion most commonly experienced when using the report and its data.

It is important to find a balance between including too much information and too little information on score reports (Sabbah, 2011). The past two decades have generated an abundance of recommendations concerning text that can be added to reports or data systems to help education stakeholders analyze data more effectively. These are wise considerations to make (e.g., ask, "Will following this recommendation for this particular report for its particular audience help its users better analyze and use the report's data, and where should the added text be placed?"). However, you do not want to adhere to all of these inclusion recommendations. In other words, do not add a footer that contains every piece of report information that a user could want to know).

Some of the added textual information would work best in the report's label (title or footer), some in its supporting documentation (reference sheet or reference guide, covered in the next chapter), some in the help system (covered in a later chapter), and some should not be included at all. Rather, you want to be familiar with the inclusion recommendations and consider them along with other evidence, such as that concerning the need to:

- not overwhelm users;
- not cause clutter;
- not include so much text that it is deemed cumbersome and ignored, etc.

Essentially, you will want to find balance in the footer, which the combination of footer standards will help you to do. Footers or other annotations on reports should include information that is crucial for users to correctly understand and interpret the data, and this text should not include any information that does not directly impact analysis. For example, 60 percent of teachers in a study had difficulty explaining a term used in a score report; thus supporting text explaining the term should be added to that report (Zapata-Rivera & VanWinkle, 2010).

- See **Examples** A and B in the "Package/Display Standards: Report Design" chapter (in color online). The scores displayed factor into a proficiency determination based on multiple criteria. Users of

Example A (Before) would have to guess at these criteria. In Example B (After), however, the criteria are noted concisely in a footer, as is the proficiency's role in considering the student for reclassification, which is indicated in a column added to display the proficiency determination. Thus educators using Example B (After) will not have to wonder why a student is or is not considered proficient, or how this impacts reclassification.

- See **Examples** E and F in the "Package/Display Standards: Report Design" chapter (in color online). Example E (Before) gives users no way to know how to spot possible site strengths and weaknesses—something educators should be able to quickly garner from this report (containing one of multiple measures used). Example F (After), however, uses a footer to concisely let users know this vital information.

Standard 1.2.03: Follow Length Guidelines (Short)

Establish and utilize system-wide guidelines concerning footer length that are followed with minimal (if any) exceptions, noting users are likely to ignore lengthy text. For example, landscape/horizontally orientated reports might have footers of up to 328 characters (including spaces), and portrait/vertically orientated reports might have footers of up to 243 characters (including spaces).

Provide details, but keep them as concise as possible (Tufte, 2011). Since users are likely to ignore a footer that is overly verbose, you should also establish and utilize system-wide (meaning for all reports in your report suite) footer guidelines concerning length. These guidelines should be followed with minimal (if any) exceptions. For example, footers on landscape/horizontally orientated reports might be kept to a maximum of 328 characters (including spaces), and footers on portrait/vertically orientated reports might be kept to a maximum of 243 characters (including spaces).

The Rankin (2013) study was used to measure the impact of two different footer formats on horizontally orientated reports and found both footer lengths led to a 307–336 percent increase in educators' data analysis accuracy. In other words, there were no significant differences between using one of these footer formats as opposed to another; each rendered accuracy increases:

- **Footer Format A1** (shorter format, 1st report used): 39 words, 186 characters without spaces, 224 characters with spaces;

- **Footer Format A2** (shorter format, 2nd report used): 34 words, 156 characters without spaces, 228 characters with spaces;

- **Footer Format B1** (longer format, 1st report used): 58 words, 269 characters without spaces, 324 characters with spaces;

- **Footer Format B2** (longer format, 2nd report used): 42 words, 199 characters without spaces, 237 characters with spaces.

Note all footers used in the study were concise, as footers should be as concise as possible. Even though some users might not know about the importance of sample size or understand the distinction between significant vs. insignificant differences, you cannot attempt to teach a full statistics course within a footer. The footer should be a place where the most important information for analyses of the report's data can stand alone and be seen.

When a lot of information is crucial to users avoiding common analysis mistakes for a particular dataset (i.e., if you find yourself wanting to go past your footer length limits), consider using one the following solutions.

Indicate There Is More Than Meets the Eye

Give users enough information to know there is more to the data than meets the eye. Even if a user does not thoroughly understand the footer's minimal explanation, he or she will at least know that more information is needed and will be encouraged to consult additional resources before continuing with an analysis approach he or she can now see was more simplistic than is needed.

You might direct users to the report's reference sheet or reference guide, covered in the "Supplemental Documentation Standards" chapter of this book. However, be sure to also include the part of the footer noted above (letting users know there is more to the data than meets the eye), since

> **Example:** Consider the footer example given at the start of this chapter. You might want to simplify it like this:
>
> > **Warning:** Clusters vary in difficulty, so the School's highest percent correct is not necessarily a strength. Subtract State Minimally Proficient percent to judge School performance. See report's reference sheet for guidance.

people are not likely to seek out the additional resource unless they know it is crucial. While many will likely be viewing the report in printed form, this mention of the resource can be featured as a hyperlink for users viewing the report directly in the data system (i.e., one click will take them directly to the report's reference sheet or reference guide).

Direct Users to Other Resources

Direct users to other resources, such as a website where concepts are explained in full. This is not a good solution for cases like the above example where most people analyze the data incorrectly . . . and without knowing they are analyzing the data incorrectly. Those people simply will not seek out the additional resources. However, this is a good approach for cases where the added information can help guide the data's use or improve an understanding of the data's source *but* is not crucial to users avoiding a flawed analysis. See the example on the next page.

Extend End-of-Report Footer

Consider a distinction between bottom-of-each-page footers and end-of-report footers. When a report is multiple pages long, consider a very short footer at the bottom of each page that lets users know there is more to the data than meets the eye (as with the example above on footers), but also mention in the footer that a detailed explanation is featured on the last page of the report (then put one there).

Label Standards

> **Example:** If even novice data users can easily judge which students are proficient vs. which are not on a report (e.g., the report reads either "Proficient" or "Not Proficient" next to each student's name), but users commonly struggle with understanding how this proficiency status was determined, or knowing how to help students based on this proficiency status, the footer or supplemental documentation (covered in the next chapter) could refer users to a website or online handbook to help with these matters. While many will likely be viewing the report in printed form, this mention of the resource can also be featured as a hyperlink for users viewing the report directly in the data system (i.e., one click will take them directly to the website or online handbook mentioned).

Standard 1.2.04: Follow Font Guidelines (Same Size/Type as Report's Data)

Establish and utilize system-wide guidelines requiring the footer's font size to be the same as that used for most data in the report (resist the urge to make the footer smaller). Also use the same font type whenever appropriate.

It is helpful to establish and utilize system-wide footer guidelines concerning font size. For example, since users attribute reduced importance to text in font sizes that are smaller than that used elsewhere on a report, the font size should be the same size as most data on the report (otherwise, users will often ignore it, rejecting its potential to help their analyses). It should also be the same (or similar) font to avoid visual dissonance. For example, if the report's data is displayed in size 10 Arial font, the footer should be displayed in size 10 Arial font. Remember:

> Users who are analyzing the data incorrectly often *do not know* they are analyzing the data incorrectly.

Thus a data system should not allow its footers to be easily overlooked. This concept is developed further in the "Size Reflects Importance" section of the "Package/Display Standards: Report Design" chapter of this book.

41

References

Aschbacher, P. R., & Herman, J. L. (1991). *Guidelines for effective score reporting: CSE Technical Report 326.* Los Angeles, CA: UCLA Center for Research on Evaluation, Standards, and Student Testing.

Few, S. (2006, February). *Common pitfalls in dashboard design.* Boise, ID: ProClarity Corporation.

Hattie, J. (2010). Visibly learning from reports: The validity of score reports. *Online Educational Research Journal.* Retrieved from www.oerj.org/View?action=view Paper&paper=6 (accessed October 30, 2015).

James-Ward, C., Fisher, D., Frey, N., & Lapp, D. (2013). *Using data to focus instructional improvement.* Alexandra, VA: ASCD.

Metropolitan Life Insurance Company (2013). *MetLife survey of the American teacher: Challenges for school leadership.* New York, NY: Author and Peanuts Worldwide.

Rankin, J. G. (2013). *Over-the-counter data's impact on educators' data analysis accuracy.* ProQuest Dissertations and Theses, 3575082. Retrieved from http://pqdtopen.proquest.com/doc/1459258514.html?FMT=ABS (accessed October 30, 2015).

Sabbah, F. M. (2011). *Designing more effective accountability report cards.* ProQuest Dissertations and Theses, AAT 3469488. Retrieved from http://search.proquest.com/docview/893068662 (accessed October 30, 2015).

Tufte, E. (2011, December 8). *Presenting data and information.* Presentation conducted from the Westin San Francisco Market Street, San Francisco, CA.

Underwood, J. (2013). *Data visualization best practices.* Retrieved from www.slideshare.net/idigdata/data-visualization-best-practices-2013 (accessed October 30, 2015).

Zapata-Rivera, D., & VanWinkle, W. (2010). A research-based approach to designing and evaluating score reports for teachers. *ETS Research Memorandum RM-10-01. Princeton,* NJ: ETS.

3 | Supplemental Documentation Standards

Definition of Supplemental Documentation

Supplemental documentation accompanies each data report to ensure educators read the report properly, understand its data, and are primed to use the data properly. Data that is "over-the-counter" provides users with access to two types of supplemental documentation (accessible in printed and digital form):

- A **reference sheet**—often called an abstract—is a single page that accompanies a report in order to help the educator more easily understand the report (shown later in this chapter).
- A **reference guide**—also called an interpretation guide—is a packet of two or more pages that accompanies a report in order to help the educator more easily use the report (shown later in this chapter).

The reference sheet and reference guide help support educators of varied data analysis proficiency and comfort levels, as well as varied technical skills and comfort levels.

Supplemental documentation is an ideal location for report-specific information that educators need but which cannot fit into the report's label, which must remain concise so as to not overwhelm readers. Again, we can see how the makers of over-the-counter medicine support users with both forms of help. When a medication label is not large enough to accommodate all information the consumer needs to use the contents properly, a folded-up piece of paper or pamphlet is enclosed within the package to offer further explanation on the product's use. Reference

43

Supplemental Documentation Standards

sheets and reference guides provide that type of added support for education report users.

How to Implement Supplemental Documentation Standards

Resources

Access the following:

- OTCD *Supplemental Documentation* standards (on pages 2–3 of OTCD Standards)
- Details on research-based evidence supporting *Supplemental Documentation* standards
- Free templates to help you create reference sheets and reference guides
- Samples of reference sheets and reference guides used by others (e.g., by researcher, by vendor, by district, and by state department of education)

An ideal data reporting environment should reflect the OTCD *Supplemental Documentation* standards, which stipulate research-based ways data systems/reports can provide reference sheets and reference guides. These standards can be found online with details on the extensive research informing every standard.

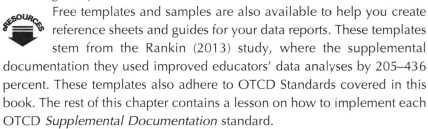

Free templates and samples are also available to help you create reference sheets and guides for your data reports. These templates stem from the Rankin (2013) study, where the supplemental documentation they used improved educators' data analyses by 205–436 percent. These templates also adhere to OTCD Standards covered in this book. The rest of this chapter contains a lesson on how to implement each OTCD *Supplemental Documentation* standard.

> ### Real-World Implementation: Supplemental Documentation
>
> **By Dr. Margie L. Johnson, Business Intelligence Coordinator, Metro Nashville Public Schools (MNPS)**
>
> When educational organizations purchase your technology product for data dissemination, do not assume that educators know what the data mean. In a study by Dr. Jenny Rankin, only 11 percent of educators were able to accurately analyze a simple bar graph of data. I dare to say that inaccurate analysis of data in any organization leads to wasted resources.
>
> A great way to support educators proactively to use your technology product (data system) is to provide built-in supports, such as supplemental documentation. The supplemental documentation is a cost-effective way to provide job-embedded data literacy and analysis support within the data system and differentiate you from the competition.
>
> We designed data guides for our district's data warehouse based off of Dr. Jenny Rankin's work (OTCD). I adapted them a bit for our needs, such as changing the name to data guide. The feedback from meeting with central office teams has been positive, and the guides have helped build capacity throughout the district to ensure the data are used appropriately for making informed decisions that increase student achievement.

Reference Sheets

Standard 2.1.01: Present

Provide a reference sheet for every report, explaining that specific report. Include the sheet even for simple reports to offer users assurance/consistency.

Not all pertinent information about analyzing a particular report's data can fit in the report's title and label (covered in the previous chapter). Trying

Supplemental Documentation Standards

to cram in too much information would make report titles less effective and would make users less likely to read report footers. Too much information or text can overwhelm users and cause them to miss higher-level implications (Hattie, 2010; VanWinkle et al., 2011; Zapata-Rivera & VanWinkle, 2010).

Data reporting environments can pair data with a reference sheet for each report, offering further explanation that typically cannot fit in places like the footer (covered in the previous chapter). The reference sheet offers report-specific details such as information about the test or data source, the report's purpose and focus, and how to avoid common misunderstandings about the data.

Research indicates that viewing a report's reference sheet before using the report can significantly improve chances of analyzing the report's data appropriately. The reference sheet is particularly helpful for the kinds of educator who want more support in understanding a report and its data, but who do not have a lot of time and/or do not want to muddle through a lot of text (i.e., dislike reference guides, which are longer and covered in the next section).

In the 211-educator Rankin (2013) study described earlier, where data analysis accuracy in the control group (without reference sheets) was only 11 percent:

- Educators whose data reports were accompanied by reference sheets used the reference sheets 50 percent of the time.
- In terms of relative and absolute differences, educators' analyses of data were 205 percent more accurate (with a 12 percentage point difference) when a reference sheet was present and 300 percent more accurate (with a 22 percentage point difference) when respondents specifically indicated having used the reference sheet.

The reference sheets used in the Rankin (2013) study followed OTCD Standards covered in this book and match available templates. Sample reference sheets are also provided online.

Reference sheets' likelihood of improving educators' data analyses by 205–300 percent makes this reference tool a key component to making data reports work for educators. Each report to which a user has access (as many reports are role- or region-specific) should have a reference sheet to go with that report, meaning the reference sheet is specific to that report.

46

A very simple and straightforward report can have a very simple and straightforward reference sheet, but even a simple report should have a reference sheet. Some users will use the reference sheet before generating a report to determine if the report will meet their needs; thus even a simple report's reference sheet can serve an important function. Also, users will grow accustomed to having one reference sheet per report, so at the very least a reference sheet for a simple report will assure the report's user that there are no overlooked complexities in the report. For reports communicating more complex data, the reference sheet becomes even more important.

Standard 2.1.02: Accessible

Make the sheet easily accessible with an obvious report-to-sheet link and with PDF downloading and printing capabilities.

Given how busy educators are, they will only use (and thus benefit from) reference sheets if the sheets are extremely easy to access. For example, users might be:

- emailing specific reports to their educator colleagues, in which case they should be able to email the URLs for accompanying reference sheets to them or attach the sheets to the email;
- handing printed reports to their educator colleagues, in which case they should be able to hand them the accompanying reference sheets (printed).

Given that 44 percent of educators use data systems directly for generating reports to analyze student data (Underwood et al., 2008), it is ideal to also make reference sheets available electronically, as well as make them printable and downloadable:

- Data systems or online/computerized collections of reports should offer an easy-to-spot link, which users can click while viewing a report, to immediately access the report's reference sheet.
- When viewing reference sheets on the computer/web, users should be able to download the sheets as Adobe PDF files (to save, email, etc.) and print them.

47

Standard 2.1.03: Helpful Contents

Include helpful contents such as: (a) title at the top of the reference sheet matching the title of the report, with the nature of the sheet ("Reference Sheet") underneath; (b) description of the sheet's purpose and any abbreviations used; and (c) a reduced image of what the report generally looks like when it has been generated (images can be "stacked" to show multiple report pages with significant differences); as well as sections for (d) "Purpose" (answering, "What are some questions this report will help answer?"; (e) "Focus" (answering, "Who is the intended audience?" "What data is reported?", and "How is the data reported?"); and (f) "Warning" (answering, "What do many educators misunderstand?" in a way that helps users overcome mistakes most likely to be made when analyzing this report's data).

Reference sheet samples and recommendations vary widely in terms of contents, and recommendations can be overwhelming. The reference sheets used in the Rankin (2013) study followed OTCD Standards covered in this book and match available templates. Tested reference sheets included key content categories used to manage appropriate information (numbers below refer to numbers on Figure 3.1):

1 **Title** at the top of the reference sheet matches the title of the report. Notice how it is offset from the term *Reference Sheet* to reduce clutter around the title.

2 **Description** explains the sheet's purpose and any abbreviations (used in the report) for those who need them.

3 **Image** shows what the report typically looks like when it has been generated. If the report has multiple pages that look significantly different, they are included (it is fine to "stack" the images so only parts of subsequent report images show). This will help users know which report to use the sheet with, and in cases where they are viewing the reference sheet before generating the report it will help them decide if it is the report they want.

4 **Purpose** answers, "What are some questions this report will help answer?" After this follows a list of 3–6 specific, common questions users might have that this report is specifically designed to answer. Actual

48

Supplemental Documentation Standards

❶ CST Performance Report
Reference Sheet

This page provides an abstract for the *CST Performance* report, which shows a school site's performance on California ❷ Standards Test (CST) content clusters in relation to the state's performance (scores of students statewide who scored *Proficient* on the CST).

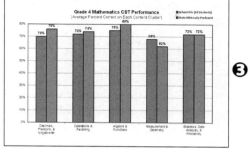

❸

❹ Purpose What are some questions this report will help answer?

- What are possible weaknesses for my school site (in a grade and subject area)?
- What are possible strengths for my school site (in a grade and subject area)?
- Which content clusters were assessed with the hardest questions on this CST?
- Which content clusters were assessed with the easiest questions on this CST?

❺ Focus Who is the intended audience?

Teachers and administrators

What data is reported?

Students' average % correct when answering questions aligned to each CST content cluster is displayed for:
- a school site
- the State Minimally Proficient (meaning all students in California who scored the minimum scale score needed—350—to be considered *Proficient* on this CST)

How is the data reported?

The school site is graphed in blue, and the State Minimally Proficient is graphed in orange.

❻ Warning What do many educators misunderstand?

Content clusters vary in difficulty, so a site's highest % correct for a cluster does not necessarily indicate its strength, and its lowest % correct for a cluster is not necessarily its weakness. For each cluster, compare the Site % to the State Minimally Proficient % (i.e., *look at the degree to which the Site beat the State Minimally Proficient*). Use this formula:

<u>School Site %</u> – <u>State Minimally Proficient %</u> = #

The cluster with the highest difference (highest # from above formula) could be a Site strength, and the cluster with the lowest difference (lowest # from above formula) could be a Site weakness.

Figure 3.1

questions may be infinite, so this section tries to capture the most common, and users can look for questions similar or related to their own.

5 **Focus** addresses who the report is meant for and what data these users will see reported. This section provides answers to the questions, "Who is the intended audience?", "What data is reported?", and "How is the data reported?"

Supplemental Documentation Standards

6 **Warning** is often the most important section of the sheet. It answers the question, "What do many educators misunderstand?" and can relate to mistakes they are most likely to make when analyzing this report's data, an inappropriate way in which educators often try to use this report's data, etc. Referencing pertinent Family Education Rights and Privacy Act (FERPA) Regulations here can be helpful for some reports.

See details on the extensive research informing every standard. There is an overwhelming number of research-based recommendations for added information that should accompany reports. The reference sheet is one place that pertinent information for a particular report should go, so that the report itself can remain as uncluttered as possible. However, cautions against information-overload are equally prevalent. When including contents, keep your reference sheet straightforward and concise so it remains effective.

Standard 2.1.04: Follow Consistency Guidelines

Remain consistent in (a) appearance (e.g., order of info, layout, color choices, etc.) and (b) content type (e.g., users can expect the same types of info from each reference sheet).

Educators will have an easier time using reference sheets (with skills transferring from past experience with one reference sheet to new experience with the next) if the reference sheets are consistent in:

- **appearance** (e.g., layout, order of information, color choices, etc.);
- **content** (e.g., after using a reference sheet for one report, educators know they can expect the same types of information in reference sheets for other reports).

Thus you (or anyone else designing the sheets, such as an educator with which you are collaborating) will need to decide ahead of time what these consistency guidelines will be. View multiple reports to be sure the guidelines will lend themselves well to all reports.

At the same time, however, use common sense when following guidelines. If it would be unnecessary and ridiculous to conform to a guideline

50

Supplemental Documentation Standards

> **Example:** If in answer to the question "What do many educators misunderstand?" you typically address a data analysis misstep, yet for one report the problem more commonly lies with an inappropriate way in which educators often try to *use* the report's data, include help for the latter (more common) problem.

for a particular report, allow for slight variations on a rare basis. See the example above.

If you intend to implement reference sheets first (e.g., for all reports) and then implement reference guides (covered in the next section) at a later time, establish consistency guidelines for both reference sheets and reference guides ahead of time. Otherwise, when the time comes to create the data system's reference guides, the reference sheets might need to be revised (causing extra work). As with most additions to a report suite or data system, it is good to plan ahead.

The concept of consistency is developed further in the "Design Consistency" section of the "Package/Display Standards: User Interface" chapter of this book. More information on reference sheet content decisions is also available earlier in this chapter.

Reference Guides

Standard 2.2.01: Present

Provide a reference guide for every report, explaining that specific report. Include the guide even for simple reports to offer users assurance/ consistency.

Like reference sheets, research shows value in reference guides, which are like extended versions of the reference sheets. The reference guide is a two- or three-page guide that accompanies a report in order to help the educator more easily use the particular report and analyze its data. The guide is particularly helpful for the kinds of educator who want extended help in using a report.

For example, while the reference sheet might tell users that a report *can* answer the question of, "Which school in my district showed the most improvement in Mathematics on the state test this year?" the reference guide will show exactly *how* to use the report to answer that particular question (e.g., where to look on the report, what pieces of data to compare there, what the implications are if a number there is red vs. green, etc.). Reference guides provide more handholding for educators who need it, and they also provide deeper explanations for advanced users who want more specific details.

Reference guides are a good place for some of the research-based recommendations for information that should accompany reports. This is largely due to the need to avoid information-overload within reports, though information should also be carefully selected for guides. Only information best suited for each report's guide should be included, based on a report's user's most likely needs.

In the 211-educator Rankin (2013) study described earlier, where data analysis accuracy in the control group (without reference guides) was only 11 percent:

- Educators whose data reports were accompanied by reference guides used the reference guides 52 percent of the time.

- In terms of relative and absolute differences, educators' analyses of data were 273 percent more accurate (with a 19 percentage point difference) when a reference guide was present and 436 percent more accurate (with a 37 percentage point difference) when respondents specifically indicated having used the reference guide.

The reference guides used in the Rankin (2013) study followed OTCD Standards covered in this book and match available templates. Sample reference guides are also provided online.

Reference guides' likelihood of improving educators' data analyses by 273–436 percent makes this reference tool a key component to making data reports work for educators. The simplest way to describe a reference guide is that it is like a reference sheet, only more detailed and thus longer. When it is present for educators using a data report, the reference guide can walk users through the report's data interpretation and use. This is an added bonus the reference sheet lacks.

A reference guide can contain the same information as the report's reference sheet (as is recommended for the guide's first page) but go further. The reference guide's additional pages show users how to read the report, how to use the report to answer specific questions, and/or where to go for more information on related topics. Though it is less pertinent to include the reference guide for simple reports than it is to include reference sheets for simple reports, the provision of reference guides for all reports offers consistency and can assure users they are on the right track when using reports.

Standard 2.2.02: Accessible

Make the guide easily accessible with an obvious report-to-guide link and with PDF downloading and printing capabilities.

Given how busy educators are, they will only use (and thus benefit from) reference guides if the guides are extremely easy to access:

- Data systems or online/computerized collections of reports should offer an easy-to-spot link, which users can click while viewing a report, to immediately access the report's reference guide.
- When viewing reference guides on the computer/web, users should be able to download the guides as PDF files (to save, email to others, etc.) and print them.

The sheets should support the varied ways in which educators can use sheets:

- Some users might email specific reports to their colleagues, in which case they should be able to email the URLs for accompanying reference sheets to them or attach the sheets to the email.
- Other users might hand printed reports to their colleagues, in which case they should be able to hand them the accompanying reference sheets (printed).

Remember that 56 percent of educators do not use data systems directly (e.g., others generate reports on their behalf) (Underwood et al., 2008). Thus educators still using printed formats need to be accommodated.

Supplemental Documentation Standards

Standard 2.2.03: Helpful Contents

Include helpful sections such as: (a) reference sheet (as described in Standard 2.1.03) as the reference guide's first page, followed by sections for (b) "Instructions" answering/illustrating, "How do I read the report?"; (c) "Essential Questions" answering/illustrating each question listed under "Purpose: What are some questions . . . " on the guide's first page; and (d) "More Info" answering questions that lead users to additional info on related topics.

The goal of the reference guide is not to teach the user about data analysis in general. For example, the guide should not try to communicate the importance of using multiple measures to make a decision rather than merely relying on one report's data. Such an education could fill a book, would overwhelm the user, and would cause clutter in which attributes important to analyzing the particular report's data would be lost.

Rather, reference guides should only include information specific to the particular report with which it is paired. Guidance not specific to the report—such as the importance of using multiple measures—can go in the help system (covered in the next chapter). For example, supplemental documentation can address all important information that cannot fit in the footer, while also expounding upon the footer's brief statement(s) and upon information provided in the report's reference sheet.

The reference guides used in the Rankin (2013) study followed OTCD Standards covered in this book and match available templates. Tested reference guides included key content categories used to manage appropriate information (numbers below refer to numbers on Figures 3.2–3.4):

1   The same information included in the **reference sheet** (discussed in the previous section) should also constitute the first page of the reference guide. The data system could still offer the one-page reference sheet elsewhere in the system (e.g., a separate link) for those who only want that one page of information, but the reference sheet's content also functions well as the grounding information the reference guide needs. This way the two do not get separated (e.g., the reference sheet's information should not be left out of the reference guide with the expectation that people will also access and view the reference sheet, because they often will not, and the result will be that people needing the extended help of the guide will be confused).

54

Supplemental Documentation Standards

CST Performance Report
❷ Reference Guide

This 3-page guide explains the *CST Performance* report, which shows a school site's performance on California Standards Test (CST) content clusters in relation to the state's performance (scores of students statewide who scored *Proficient* on the CST).

❶

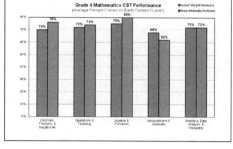

Purpose What are some questions this report will help answer?

- What are possible weaknesses for my school site (in a grade and subject area)?
- What are possible strengths for my school site (in a grade and subject area)?
- Which content clusters were assessed with the hardest questions on this CST?
- Which content clusters were assessed with the easiest questions on this CST?

Focus Who is the intended audience?

Teachers and administrators

What data is reported?

Students' average % correct when answering questions aligned to each CST content cluster is displayed for:
- a school site
- the State Minimally Proficient (meaning all students in California who scored the minimum scale score needed—350—to be considered *Proficient* on this CST)

How is the data reported?

The school site is graphed in blue, and the State Minimally Proficient is graphed in orange.

Warning What do many educators misunderstand?

Content clusters vary in difficulty, so a site's highest % correct for a cluster does not necessarily indicate its strength, and its lowest % correct for a cluster is not necessarily its weakness. For each cluster, compare the Site % to the State Minimally Proficient % (i.e., *look at the degree to which the Site beat the State Minimally Proficient*). Use this formula:

<u>School Site %</u> − <u>State Minimally Proficient %</u> = #

The cluster with the highest difference (highest # from above formula) could be a Site strength, and the cluster with the lowest difference (lowest # from above formula) could be a Site weakness.

❸

Figure 3.2

2 However, the guide's **heading** now clearly reads *Reference Guide* on its first page.

3 **Page Numbers** (e.g., *Pg. 1 of 3*) should be featured inobtrusively since reference guides are multiple pages. This will help users know if they are missing pages or if the pages get out of order, as can happen if the guide is printed and used as a handout.

Supplemental Documentation Standards

④ Instructions How do I read the report?

The bars show you the % of questions students answered correctly when answering questions aligned to each CST content cluster. %s above blue bars are results of students at the School Site, and %s above orange bars are results of students statewide who scored the minimum scale score needed (350) to be considered *Proficient* on this CST.

Example: The State Minimally Proficient students *and* the School Site's students both answered 72% of Qs correctly in this CST's *Statistics* cluster.

⑤ Essential What are possible weaknesses for my school site (in a grade and subject area)?

Determine the cluster in which you most lagged behind the State Minimally Proficient's (SMP's) students (or beat them to the least degree). Since clusters vary in difficulty, SMP %s account for how easy or hard the clusters were. Use this formula:

School % − SMP % = #

Example: For the *Decimals* cluster:
School 70% − SMP 76% = −6

More than for any other cluster, Site did most poorly on the *Decimals* cluster (because of how Site compared to SMP). The *Decimals* cluster is most likely Site's weakness, even though the Site's 70% for *Decimals* was not its lowest %.

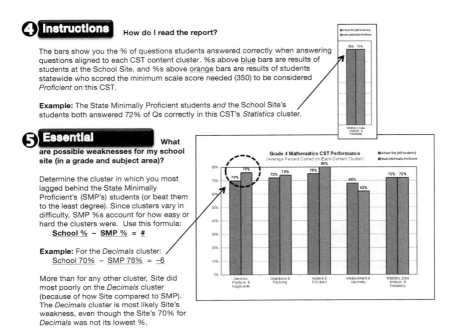

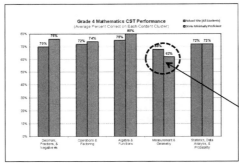

What are possible strengths for my school site (in a grade and subject area)?

Determine the cluster in which you beat the State Minimally Proficient's (SMP's) students to the greatest degree. Since clusters vary in difficulty, SMP %s account for how easy or hard the clusters were. Use this formula:

School % − SMP % = #

Example: For the *Measurement* cluster:
School 68% − SMP 62% = +6

More than for any other cluster, Site performed best on the *Measurement* cluster (because of how Site compared to SMP). The *Measurement* cluster is most likely Site's strength, even though the Site's 68% for *Measurement* was not its highest %.

Figure 3.3

4. **Instructions** provide an answer to, "How do I read this report?", and then illustrate the explanation with an example.

5. **Essential Questions** walks the user through the process of how to use the report to answer each of the questions posed in the "Purpose" section of the first page. For example, the following provides users with guidance for each question:

    – The question is repeated in bold so it functions well as a subsection's heading and is easy to spot when users visually scan the sheet.

Supplemental Documentation Standards

Which content clusters were assessed with the hardest questions on this CST?

Find the State Minimally Proficient (SMP) lowest %. Since SMP %s are the average % of questions answered correctly by all students in California who scored the minimum scale score needed – 350 – to be considered *Proficient* on this CST, clusters they struggled with the most had the hardest questions.

Example: SMP's 62% in *Measurement* is lower than the 76%, 74%, 80%, and 72% SMP earned in the other clusters. Thus the *Measurement* cluster was likely assessed with the hardest questions.

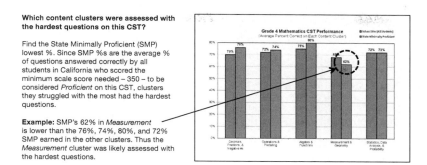

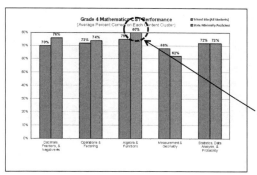

Which content clusters were assessed with the easiest questions on this CST?

Find the State Minimally Proficient (SMP) highest %. Clusters that SMP had the easiest time with had the easiest questions.

Example: SMP's 80% in *Algebra* is higher than the 76%, 74%, 62%, and 72% SMP earned in the other clusters. Thus the *Algebra* cluster was likely assessed with the easiest questions.

⑥ More Info Where can I find more info on the CST and its proper analysis?

Reference Chapter 1 of the *California Standardized Testing and Reporting (STAR) Post-Test Guide* at http://www.startest.org/archive.html.

Where can I find more info on analyzing CST content clusters?

Visit the Help system's *Data Analysis* manual.

Where can I learn how to generate this report in my data system?

Visit the Help system's *Reports* manual.

Figure 3.4

Remember users will not necessarily want to use the report to answer every question the report is designed to answer. Many will have a particular question in mind and thus will skim the guide to use only information pertaining directly to that question.

– An explanation is given for how the educator should use the report (e.g., where to look on the report and what to do with the data found there) to answer the given question.

Supplemental Documentation Standards

- The explanation is illustrated with snapshots of the report, arrows and circles to call attention to different areas, etc.

- An example is given.

6 **More Info** shows the user how/where to get additional information on such topics as finding additional analysis guidance, and/or help generating this report in the data system. Many report users unnecessarily rely on other people to generate and print reports for them, whereas report-generating guidance could empower them.

The information added to each guide should be written by someone intimately familiar with using the report's specific data and with extensive experience as an educator. This data reporting expert might be you or an educator with whom you are collaborating.

Standard 2.2.04: Follow Consistency Guidelines

Remain consistent in (a) appearance (e.g., order of info, layout, color choices, etc.) and (b) content type (e.g., users can expect the same types of info from each reference guide).

Unlike reference sheets, the number of pages needed for each reference guide will vary based on the complexity of the report with which it is paired, how many key questions can be answered by the report (and are thus addressed in the guide), etc. However, educators will have an easier time using reference guides that are consistent in:

- **appearance** (e.g., layout, order of information, color choices, etc.);
- **content** (e.g., after using a reference guide for one report, educators know they can expect the same types of information in guides for other reports).

This is because users' skills can transfer from experience with one guide to the user's experience with the next. You and/or anyone else designing the guides, such as any educators who have volunteered to help, will need to decide ahead of time what these consistency guidelines will be. Consider using the research-based templates and sample guides featured online, and

58

Supplemental Documentation Standards

let them inform your guidelines for reference guide appearance and content. These templates render guides that look like those on the previous pages.

View multiple reports to be sure the guidelines will lend themselves well to all reports, and share guide mockups with key stakeholders for feedback. As with reference sheets, however, use common sense when following guidelines. If it would be unnecessary and ridiculous to conform to a guideline on a particular report's reference guide, feel free to break the rules sparingly. The concept of consistency is developed further in the "Design Consistency" section of the "Package/Display Standards: User Interface" chapter of this book.

References

Hattie, J. (2010). Visibly learning from reports: The validity of score reports. *Online Educational Research Journal*. Retrieved from www.oerj.org/View?action=viewPaper&paper=6 (accessed October 30, 2015).

Rankin, J. G. (2013). *Over-the-counter data's impact on educators' data analysis accuracy*. ProQuest Dissertations and Theses, 3575082. Retrieved from http://pqdtopen.proquest.com/doc/1459258514.html?FMT=ABS) (accessed October 30, 2015).

Underwood, J. S., Zapata-Rivera, D., & VanWinkle, W. (2008). Growing pains: Teachers using and learning to use IDMS. *ETS Research Memorandum RM-08-07*. Princeton, NJ: ETS.

VanWinkle, W., Vezzu, M., & Zapata-Rivera, D. (2011). Question-based reports for policymakers. *ETS Research Memorandum RM-11-16*. Princeton, NJ: ETS.

Zapata-Rivera, D., & VanWinkle, W. (2010). A research-based approach to designing and evaluating score reports for teachers. *ETS Research Memorandum RM-10-01*. Princeton, NJ: ETS.

4 | Help System Standards

Definition of Help System

A help system embedded within a data system helps educators use the data system and appropriately analyze the data it contains. Data that is "over-the-counter"—and thus easy to use appropriately—provides users with an online help system containing two types of lesson:

- **Technical lessons** illustrate how to use the data system or other technical reporting tool (e.g., what to click for varied tasks); these lessons are generally task-based and are somewhat common in data reporting environments.

- **Data analysis lessons** communicate key data analysis topics and practices (e.g., how to determine statistical significance); these lessons are generally topic-based and are rare in data reporting environments.

The lessons offer support to educators of varied technical and data proficiency levels, particularly when they are alone (such as working from home). Lessons can also be used in conjunction with formalized PD, such as that provided by users' districts.

In the medical field, we can see how a help system is a vital over-the-counter component. Every year, approximately fifty million different people use WebMD (the WebMD Health Network, found at www.WebMD.com) (Kronstadt et al., 2009). Even when medication features effective labeling and supplemental documentation, its users still crave the convenience of an online help system where they can run searches, explore topics, and find answers to their questions. The same is true of data system users.

Educator-delivered interventions to train and support staff are not working; to truly integrate edtech, teachers need access to immediate help wherever they are using technology (O'Hanlon, 2013).

How to Implement Help System Standards

Resources

Access the following:

- OTCD *Help System* standards (on pages 4–5 of OTCD Standards)
- Details on research-based evidence supporting OTCD *Help System* standards

An ideal data reporting environment should reflect the OTCD *Help System* standards, which stipulate research-based ways data systems can provide a help system. These standards can be found online with details on the extensive research informing every standard. The rest of this chapter contains a lesson on how to implement each OTCD *Help System* standard.

Real-World Implementation: Help System (Tech Lessons)

By Ryan Winter, President, LinkIt!

As a solution provider and as a partial owner of our company, I certainly believe our product provides a simple and easy-to-use interface, logical point-and-click navigation, and overall a great user experience. However, three realities have proven to us that there are obstacles preventing educators from mastering any data system. These include:

- Educators are extremely busy and often do not have time to learn new systems.

Help System Standards

- Levels of technology interest, knowledge, and comfort around the use of data varies.
- Multi-user onsite and web-based PD can frustrate both beginners and advanced users.

We have found providing access to personalized and relevant data, coupled with self-directed lessons through the combination of help documents and videos, can be the most effective support tool. Operationally, tech lessons are tangible, portable, scalable, and *cost-effective*. Our PD offerings have been so successful that we have broken them up into two categories:

a. **product training:** "Cheat sheets" with step-by-step instructions to learn the system;

b. **instructional training:** "Blueprints" with activities, questions, and action plans to integrate into day-to-day instruction with embedded professional development.

Specifically, the standards below have provided a very helpful framework to follow:

3.1.03: Include Lessons for All Users

Lessons need to be customized by role as well as by proficiency level. Every user needs to see the benefits and value proposition as well as a path to success that is plausible and reasonable.

3.1.04: Key Features and 3.1.05: Follow Consistency Guidelines

Lessons need to have structure and consistency. Targeted, task-specific lessons have proven to be an effective best practice. Visually, having graphics, arrows, and step-by-step instructions is a must.

3.1.02: Accessible

Eighty percent of questions we receive from clients can be solved by visiting the help section of the platform. Accessibility through a help icon that stores lessons in a searchable, downloadable, and printable manner has been a very effective way of improving awareness and utilization. It should not be assumed that users will get everything they need in just a few hours of training. For that reason, making a variety of support resources directly accessible is a key element of every successful implementation.

Tech Lessons (Using the System)

Standard 3.1.01: Present

Offer a comprehensive set of tech lessons to cover all common technical tasks and key technical topics.

A survey of 600 K-12 teachers revealed that 50 percent of teachers report inadequate support for using technology in the classroom, and 46 percent report they lack the training needed to use technology successfully to help

Sample Tech Lessons (Categorized)

Introduction
- Log in and Out
- Change Password
- Use the System (Overview)

Prebuilt Reports
- Find a Report
- Generate a Report
- Download/Print a Report

Training Tools
- Videos
- Trainer Toolkit (support for educators training other educators)

students (Piehler, 2014). In addition, teachers' awareness or perceptions about a data system's available infrastructure and capabilities are not in line with the actual available infrastructure; for example, statistics suggest fewer teachers believe they have access to students' performance on diagnostic tests than teachers who actually do have such access (Faria et al., 2012).

Educators cannot view data reports on their own to analyze data in a data system if they do not know how to access the reports, generate the reports, etc. Even if static reports are listed simply on a staff portal, some educators might feel intimidated or confused by how to access them.

Over one-third of educators are older than 50 and nearing retirement (Papay, Harvard Graduate School of Education, 2007). Though some of these may nonetheless be data system power users, computer technology was not likely part of their upbringing and they may struggle with edtech. Many other educators will struggle when it comes to using technology specifically for data needs. Intimidation due to unfamiliarity with technology or previous poor experience using technology can trigger an emotional filter in users that exacerbates a lack of tech proficiency.

Ideally, a report environment should be intuitive enough that users rarely have to turn to the help system for guidance. However, *intuitive* is a subjectively applied term. Lack of tech-familiarity can cause users to struggle with systems others find easy to use, and lessons on using the system work best when they cover all key cases where help is needed.

> A shorter, targeted manual or user-friendly help system causes users to need 40% less training time and to successfully complete 50% more tasks.
>
> van der Meij, 2008

A shorter, targeted manual or user-friendly help system causes users to need 40 percent less training time and to successfully complete 50 percent more tasks (Hattie, 2010; van der Meij, 2008). Given tech lessons' task-based nature, effective tech lessons can support educators using technology to analyze data while also cutting training time. Thus a help system should contain tech lessons that help educators complete tasks within the data system. Think of these lessons as a virtual tech coach or trainer who can

Help System Standards

assist educators in using the system when a live person who can help is not present.

Due to the aforementioned reasons, a help system should accompany a data system or other data reporting environment. Ideally this help system and its tech lessons are built into or embedded within any data system being used, accessible through an easy-to-spot link. However, it can also be housed outside the data system (yet still online) when a within-system link is not possible.

If this environment is technology-based, then tech lessons should be present for all common technical tasks and key technical topics. Note these lessons are just a start, as you will also want sets of lessons for other parts of your system. For example, collections of lessons that impact data reporting might include:

- **data administrator** (a set of lessons only for educators who help manage the report environment, such as by loading the data it displays);
- **custom reports** (sorting, creating, sharing, editing, finding, etc.);
- **dashboard** (customizing, using, etc.);
- **assessments** (scanning, using item banks, taking online tests, creating, sharing, editing, finding, etc.);
- **student groups** (creating, sharing, selecting to generate a report for the group, etc.);
- **gradebook**;
- **report cards**;
- and so on.

As educators continue to use tech lessons with your reporting environment, you will identify new needs (or "holes") in the tech lesson offering. Respond to these needs with new lessons and/or adjustments to existing lessons. Be wary of simply adding more and more lessons, as the lesson offering must not overwhelm the most sensitive users.

In addition, encourage your educator clients to show their colleagues how to access and use the help system and its data analysis lessons. For example, utilizing the tech lessons should be covered in PD when appropriate. Touch base with whoever oversees users' PD to encourage its inclusion. Users might not otherwise learn the lessons are there, and most will be grateful for this added resource.

65

Help System Standards

Standard 3.1.02: Accessible

Make lessons: (a) accessible online (e.g., users can share a lesson's URL with other users, Customer Support can share a lesson's URL with a user asking for help, etc.); (b) logically organized so they are easy to manually locate within the help system; (c) searchable (e.g., users can enter a term such as "generate report" within the help system and links to relevant lessons will appear); (d) with PDF downloading and printing capabilities; and (e) (in addition to the ever-present help system link) place a specific lesson link/button in each pertinent data system area (e.g., in the part of the system where users create custom reports, offer a link directly to the "Create Custom Report" lesson).

With easy access to technical lessons, educators using the data system alone will not be completely alone, as a tech expert's guidance will be in the room with them. This expert guidance can support staff in using the data system whenever the educator wants help. The help system's tech lessons are crucial to making data reports work for educators.

In order to make access easy and likely, technical help lessons should be:

Online

Housing the lessons online allows educators to easily share a lesson's URL with other users. For example, if someone is emailing a teacher about a particular report, he or she can include the URL for the lesson on how to generate that report, and doing so will not increase the size of his or her email like attaching a PDF file would. District email accounts often have limits on attachment file sizes and/or on total storage allotment for each account.

An added advantage for anyone offering technical support, such as a vendor's Customer Support team or a district's Information Technology (IT) Department, is that support staff can share a lesson's URL with an educator who calls or emails for help. This way the educator has a clearer picture of what to do than mere words could provide, and Customer Support is saved time in helping him or her. In addition, users' familiarity with the help system increases use, thus building self-sufficiency and reducing future calls for help.

Logically Organized

Lessons should be arranged in a logical order so it is easy to manually locate a needed lesson within the system. Note the way the sample lessons shown in the Standard 3.1.01 section are housed within chapters in the help system. They form a two-level outline of categorized lessons. In this case, there are very few lessons per category so they are listed based on the order in which users would likely need them. For longer lists of lessons, it is advisable to alphabetize lessons within each category.

Searchable

Educators should be able to enter terms (such as "generate report") and links to relevant lessons should appear. Boolean search capabilities—such as allowing words such as AND, OR, NOT, etc. to further refine results—are also helpful.

Figure 4.1 Search field made using ScreenSteps

Searching capabilities should be obvious to users. For example, in help systems built using ScreenSteps, the above field is always present at the top of the Help screen, where it can be used at any time.

Downloadable and Printable

When viewing a lesson, users should be able to easily download the lesson as an Adobe PDF file. This format is one that can be saved and viewed on virtually any computer operating system, as long as free Adobe software such as Adobe Acrobat has been downloaded on the computer. Visit www.adobe.com/products/acrobat/adobepdf.html for more details. Since educators often do not have access to install software on their district computers, it is wise to ensure that such software has been loaded on all computers in the district (something you and/or your staff can encourage). Otherwise, users will not be able to benefit from this useful lesson aspect. Users should also be able to easily print the lesson, such as by clicking a "Print" link or icon.

Easy to Access

While the help system should always be one click away via an ever-present *Help* button in the data system, it is also helpful if particular lessons are available via a link (such as a "?" button) within pertinent data system areas. For example, if educators are using a report's input controls, they could have the option of clicking such a button/link to reach a lesson defining input control terms, such as demographic labels and the criteria used to assign them.

Always a Possibility

If you are not someone who has control over your data system, you can still build and provide a help system for it. Consult with key stakeholders to select a help system software tool (such as ScreenSteps) at your district before working on a help system. Note the author of this book is not affiliated with ScreenSteps in any way; rather, I am a fan and user of the product. Such a tool will best allow you to conform to the *Help System* standards, as you will be able to create successful lessons quickly and easily in a format that will allow users to run searches for lessons, export lessons to PDF, view an illustration for every step, etc. It will also be easy for you to manage lessons and make quick changes when necessary. Creating static lessons using a document program such as Microsoft Word will not render the same results.

Also determine where a link to the online help system will be housed. For example, you might provide the link within the staff portal, next to the link staff uses to access the related data system. You can still work with your DSRP to house the link directly within the data system, but a location you control also works.

Working with other stakeholders will also save you time and lighten your workload when creating a help system. For example, a data coordinator might share a lesson packet she uses when coaching staff, in which case you could copy some of the content and place it within lessons you create (with appropriate consent).

Also ask your DSRP for any assorted lessons it might have (e.g., many DSRPs have "how to" sheets they hand out at trainings yet do not house online) to make this task easier. Try to get electronic copies of these so you can copy/paste content as permitted.

Standard 3.1.03: Include Lessons for All Users

Include lessons to meet all users' needs, remembering that even "intuitive" systems and processes are not intuitive to users lacking tech-familiarity. For example, some users will need a lesson on how to log into the data system.

Data system users come from varied backgrounds and all of them should be supported in ways well suited to them, just as a good teacher varies his or her instruction for varied students. For example, some users really will need a lesson on how to log into the data system. Since all lessons should be easy to download as PDF files, this would likely be a lesson that an educator leader could print and hand to an easily tech-intimidated user.

You will need to decide how the help system will be arranged in terms of manuals and chapters so that all users' needs are met and so that all types of user can easily find lessons. In *addition* to the bulk of your lessons, which should try to find middle ground in appealing to as many educators as possible, here are some level-specific ideas:

Novice Users

If you offer a large number of lessons that meet all needs but can be intimidating to new users, you might place a manual or chapter link at the top of the help system screen that says, *I'm New to Using the System* so the most easily intimidated users have the easiest time finding the lessons they need.

69

Also, within lessons, include modifiers for words that could otherwise be misunderstood by users who are not tech-savvy. For example, many such users can be confused by the term *browser*, so writing "Open your Internet browser" rather than simply "Open your browser" will provide context to aid understanding.

On this note, technical terms and actions that will not be understood by some users can be explained in a "Technical Terms" lesson included in the help system. This lesson will not need to be placed anywhere prominent, as users will not likely use it as a standalone lesson. Rather, whenever you use a term or action for which some users will need added explanation, you can feature that term as a link that leads to the explanation in the other lesson. In other words, if the user clicks the term, he or she will be taken to an explanation of the term. Opt for this explanation to occur in a new window so the new user will not lose access to the original lesson.

With this setup, you will not have to clutter your lesson with added explanations that most users will not need, but you will still be supporting users who require it. Examples of technical terms and phrases that can link to explanations elsewhere are:

- Click a <u>download</u> icon.
- <u>Drag and drop</u> your selection.
- Choose your <u>file delimiter</u> type.
- <u>Sort</u> by column.
- Open your Internet <u>browser</u>.
- Clear your Internet <u>browser's cache</u>.

Since districts' staff often lacks access to download software onto each educator's district computer, do not link software terms directly to where they may be downloaded. Link software terms to their descriptions so users can get a feel for their purpose and icons. The icons will help users find the software on their own systems, where all needed software should be installed for them, or find a download option if that will work for them.

Also link any complicated term to an online resource. Examples of terms that should link to sites outside of your help system:

- If you are using <u>Google</u> . . .
- When entering demographic codes, adhere to <u>state regulations</u> . . .
- Follow <u>FERPA Regulations</u> when . . .

Advanced Users

If lessons you create specifically for a more tech-advanced audience grow to over six, consider creating a separate chapter or manual so the lessons will not overwhelm or confuse new users. This resource can be accessible at the bottom of the chapter/manual list, or accessible via a single "Advanced Users" link. Do not underestimate your advanced users' needs.

> **Example:** District administrators might wrongfully assume teachers would never create programs (specific, non-class groups of students to report upon) in the system and thus the administrators might not want to "bother" teachers with lessons on creating and using a data system's programs feature. However, failing to include these lessons for advanced users would leave many teachers—such as those working as a grade-level team to run Response to Intervention—without guidance to help them make the most of the system and its data.

In addition to including lessons for advanced *needs*, you can save advanced users' time by providing them with abbreviated versions of regular, common-need lessons in the help system. Such a lesson—sometimes called a "Quick Teach"—uses fewer words and images to communicate steps in a task for those who do not need much support (rather, these users just need to be pointed in the right direction and can take matters from there). For example, whereas a regular lesson might read "Click *Report* at the top of your screen and then select *Prebuilt Reports* from the menu that appears," Quick Teach lesson might instead read, "Report > Prebuilt Reports".

Standard 3.1.04: Key Features

Make lessons: (a) task-specific (e.g., do not cram a single lesson with everything users might want to do in a module), with few topic-specific exceptions; (b) step by step (e.g., "1. Click *Search* in the top-right corner of your screen ... "); and (c) illustrated (e.g., show what the relevant portion of the screen looks like during each lesson segment, with numbers superimposed on the image to match numbered steps explained in the lesson, etc.).

Key features will make your tech lessons more user-friendly and more effective. Technical help lessons should be:

Task Specific

Devote tech lessons to specific tasks. For example, a single lesson should not be crammed with everything anyone might want to do in a system's *Reports* module—not even close. That cramming would overwhelm and lose the attention of a large percentage of users.

> **Example:** "Prebuilt Reports" can serve as a chapter, rather than a lesson, and then lessons within the chapter category could be provided based on specific tasks (e.g., *Find a Report, Generate a Report, Download and Print a Report*). The help system's list of lessons could then display as a tiered outline.

This organization might not seem very important when you have few tasks covered in your help system, but the number of lesson-requiring tasks will likely grow over time, making this guideline especially important.

Step by Step

Feature every click or action in the order it is performed. Complete the actual task for which you are writing a lesson, as you write it, to be sure no steps are missed. Group these steps with images, as explained below.

Illustrated

Show users what the screen or relevant portion of the screen looks like during each task or step, with numbers on the image that follow the sequence of clicks/actions being described, and with circles or arrows pointing out difficult-to-spot features. An example of steps grouped with a picture is featured below. A single lesson will typically contain multiple image+steps groupings like this:

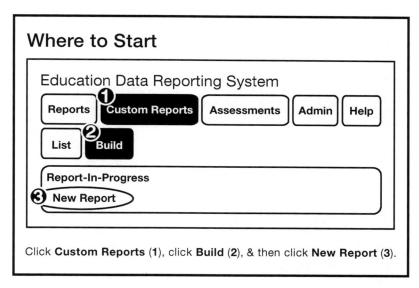

Figure 4.2

Using a single image for multiple clicks or steps helps keep the lesson to a manageable size. Despite paperless benefits, help lessons are often printed as training handouts or for reference to use while moving through the system. In these cases, shorter lessons are especially favorable.

Standard 3.1.05: Follow Consistency Guidelines

Remain consistent in (a) appearance (e.g., order of info, layout, color choices, etc.) and (b) content type (e.g., users can expect the same types of info from each of the same types of lessons).

Help System Standards

The help system's tech lessons should adhere to predetermined guidelines that keep lessons consistent in:

- **appearance** (e.g., layout, order of information, color choices, etc.);
- **content** (e.g., opening lesson description, *Where to Start* as the first step, etc.).

Lesson consistency will make it easier for users to:

- know what to look for when they are searching for a particular lesson;
- find lessons, such as by skimming the list of chapters or lessons and/or using filters to narrow down the lesson list;
- get what they want out of a lesson more quickly (e.g., they might know to always skim the "Where to Start" section, based on their ability to have already guessed the first steps of a task);
- feel an increasing sense of ease in the help system's use, as their knowledge of lessons they have used will transfer to better understanding the nature of lessons they have not yet used.

Thus you will need to decide ahead of time what these consistency guidelines will be. Consult others in this task, such as educators who will use the lessons, staff who will build the lessons, and those who train educators in using the data system. Then craft guidelines that incorporate this feedback.

Once established, these consistency guidelines will need to be thoroughly taught to anyone writing lessons for the help system so there is continuity among multiple authors' work. Understand that the guidelines you create can be broken sparingly if there is a specific and worthy reason for doing so, but this needs to be a rarity if the help system is to benefit from consistency.

Sample Guidelines

 The rest of this section features sample lesson guidelines utilized in an Illuminate Education data system's help system (all images and examples are from this help system, which I wrote with Standard 3.1.05 in mind, as created with the product ScreenSteps).

Titles

Lesson titles:

- begin with a verb (use words such as Create, Add, Edit, Manage, Find, Share, Delete, etc., e.g., *Create Custom Report*) so it is clear what the lesson will help users to do;
- are not progressive (e.g., say *Create* rather than *Creating*), as the *ing* at the end of a progressive verb would be unnecessary clutter;
- do not have any words in front of that verb (e.g., say *Create* rather than *How to Create* or *How Do I Create*), as such words would be unnecessary clutter;
- are consistent with other lessons (determine common verb choices ahead of time; e.g., if you choose to use the word *Edit* instead of *Change*, and the word *Create* as opposed to *Make*, then always do so);
- adhere to proper capitalization of titles (e.g., always capitalize first word, last word, and major words that are not articles, conjunctions, or prepositions).

Here are examples of some *exceptions* to the above rules, with parenthetical examples of their unique titling conventions:

- Frequently Asked Question (FAQ) lessons (e.g., *Custom Reporting FAQ, Demographic Labels FAQ*, etc.);
- lesson types that deviate from your other lesson formats to appeal to a unique type of learning, such as one-page abbreviated sheets for quick learners (e.g., *Quick Guide: Create Custom Report, Quick Guide: Share Report*, etc.);
- lessons that convey information but not steps (e.g., *Gradebook Features, Assessment Report Overview*, etc.);
- sequential lessons in a step-based manual, such as a help system manual titled "Implement District-Wide Common Assessments" (e.g., *Step 1. Outline a Preliminary Plan, Step 2. Form Assessment Team*, etc.).

Help System Standards

Use Guidelines Right for You

Before establishing tag guidelines, it is important to understand how tags function in the particular help system software you are using. For example, if multiple words are entered in a search, will a huge list of any lesson featuring any of its words appear, or will it only render lessons that include all words entered in a search? It is also helpful to know of any planned changes to how these tags will function in the near future. These tag guidelines featured here are those that worked for one particular help system.

Tags

Lesson **tags** facilitate users' searches for particular lessons. A user can run a search for a particular term, known as a tag, and all lessons that were tagged with that term are then listed for the user. Tag guidelines:

- Include synonyms (e.g., the lesson title reads *Create*, but someone might instead search for *Add, Make, Write*, etc., so all these should be included as tags, provided the help system narrows—rather than expands—the list of lessons when a combination of words is used in a search).

- Include other forms of each verb (e.g., add both *Make* and *Making* for a *Create* lesson, since the user could use either to search, and since the word *Make* is not featured in its entirety within the word *Making*; rather, its ending "e" is dropped).

- Add a tag for any word not anywhere in the lesson that could likely be part of a search for that lesson. See the example below.

Example: Imagine an "Enter Grades" lesson that contains the term *grade book* within its lesson content but doesn't feature the term as a closed compound (*gradebook*). If the lesson is tagged with the word *gradebook* (among other tags), when a user searches for *gradebook* in the help system, this lesson or its link will appear.

Intro

There should be an introduction at the top/beginning of a lesson that helps to describe the lesson and its purpose. The introduction should:

- give a little background (examples are also helpful) on why someone would want to use this particular lesson;
- be succinct;
- end with a straightforward statement on what the lesson will help users accomplish;
- address the user as "you."

Where to Start

Using "Where to Start" as the first task in a lesson (which means a section titled "Where to Start" and containing an image with perhaps one to three numbered steps, as shown in Figure 4.2) is reassuring to users.

- Every "how to" lesson (i.e., every lesson but an FAQ, Quick Teach/ Guide, non-technical, etc.) opens with a *Where to Start* section telling users how to get to where the lesson needs them to be (such as opening a particular module or menu in the system). This section will hold the hand of someone who has merely logged into the system and not done anything else.
- Many users will already have conducted this step using common sense, and those types of fast learners will be able to skip this section. Always calling the section *Where to Start* lets these users use the lessons more quickly, knowing which verbiage they can easily bypass. However, you need to appeal to all users' needs, so including this section will hold the hand of those who need it.
- A typical *Where to Start* section example was shown earlier for Standard 3.1.04. Notice the exact wording and how the numbered steps in the instructions correspond with the numbers in the image.
- You can modify the *Where to Start* section for cases where a lengthy process is needed to get to where the lesson begins. You do not want

more than a few steps to clutter the *Where to Start* section. Rather, a link can lead to an entire, separate lesson devoted to such lengthy steps. For example, the instructions in this step might read:

> Open the record of a student. See the "**Search for a Student**" lesson for help.

The step should display an image that still manages to point the user in the right direction (such as by displaying an area of the user's screen with circles around the links the user should click).

Middle Sections

The "Where to Start" section is generally followed by one task for each screenshot the user encounters while completing the lesson. After your Where to Start section/step(s), each new task gets a new title. Sample title guidelines for these sections:

- Sometimes this means each step gets a title, but often you need multiple steps or images per task (in which case you only title the first in a series of steps/images).
- Each step title describes an action with a non-progressive verb whenever appropriate (such as *View Your List, Filter Your List,* etc.), but they can also be a little different (e.g., *Options*).

Next Steps

It is also reassuring to end each lesson with an indication of (and link to support for) the user's next likely action after the lesson's purpose/task is completed. Thus *Next Steps* is the lesson's final section and step. Like the *Where to Start* section, many users will choose to ignore it. Conversely, many will use it. Guidelines for this section include:

- Finish the lesson with a *Next Steps* section/step that succinctly includes a likely suggestion users will commonly need at this point.
- If the next likely step is a process warranting its own lesson, include a link to that lesson.

A typical *Next Steps* example will often include a link to another lesson. For example, the section's single step might read:

> After your answer sheets print, you might want to use the **"Scan Student Responses"** lesson to score students' sheets.

Special Fonts and Word Types

Bold text should be utilized with purpose. The following are guidelines for making words bold (as opposed to in quotes or italics):

- anything users will click, select, or type (these should also be written exactly as they appear on the screen; e.g., if it is capitalized in the data system, it is capitalized in the help system);

- numbers that correspond to blue (or other color you have pre-determined) numbers used in the image; also include spaces between numbered steps if each step is a line or longer (as opposed to three quick steps you can include in a single line), and establish how the numbers will be typed: e.g., **1.** at start of each new line, or **(1)** when the step is part of a multi-step line;

- any offset **"Note:"** that alerts users to extra information;

- the word **example** when it precedes a thorough example.

Other word type guidelines include:

- Underline *if* when the sentence does not apply to everyone, e.g.: If you have not already opened your assessment, do so now. See the "Find an Assessment" lesson for more details.

- Links should be underlined and in blue, and should open in the same window if they are help system URLs and open in another window if they are URLs outside the help system.

- Include modifiers for words that could otherwise be misunderstood (e.g., many non-techies can be confused by the term *browser*, so write, "Open your Internet browser" rather than simply "Open your browser").

Describe relevant icons and characters when they are not labeled. **Examples**:

- Click the **pencil and paper** icon in front of any scope to edit the scope.
- Click the **red minus** (–) icon next to any assessment to delete it.
- Red asterisks (*) identify fields that must be populated in order to proceed.

Technical Terms

Whenever you use a term or action for which some users will need added explanation, you can feature that term as a link that leads to the explanation in another lesson (e.g., a "Technical Terms" lesson). In other words, if the user clicks the term, he or she will be taken to an explanation of the term.

This way you will not have to clutter your lesson with added explanations that most users will not need, but you will still be supporting users who require it. **Examples** of technical terms and phrases that can link to explanations elsewhere:

- Click a <u>download</u> *icon.*
- <u>Drag and drop</u> your selection.
- Choose your <u>file delimiter</u> type.
- <u>Sort</u> by column.
- Open your Internet <u>browser</u>.
- Clear your Internet <u>browser's cache</u>.

Since not all districts' staff have been granted access to download software onto their district computers, do not link software terms directly to where they may be downloaded. Link software terms to their descriptions so users can get a feel for their purpose and icons (this will help users find the software on their own systems, where all needed software should be installed for them, or find a download option if that will work for them).

- If you are using <u>Google</u> . . .
- When entering demographic codes, adhere to <u>state regulations</u> . . .
- Follow <u>FERPA Regulations</u> when . . .

Drawing Objects

Stick to predetermined guidelines for drawing objects such as circles and arrows. For example, most things users click, select, or type are circled in red, and actions are numbered when there is more than one step. Here are sample setting specifications for each:

- **Circle**
  - Border = Yes (the same shade of red shown in this step's image)
  - Fill = No
  - Border Size = 3
  - Fill Opacity = 40
  - Drop Shadow = Yes
- **Rectangle**
  - The same rules as those given for "Circle", plus:
  - Corner Radius = 15
- **Step Numbers**
  - Border/Text = Yes (white)
  - Fill = Yes (the same shade of blue shown in this step's image)
  - Border Size = 2
  - Opacity = 100
  - Step Starting Sequence = 1 (in all cases)
  - Drop Shadow = Yes
  - Text = Arial 14
- **Arrows and Lines**
  - Line Color = the same shade of red shown in this step's image
  - Start/End Arrow = whatever is needed
  - Line Size = 5
  - Arrow Size = 5
  - Drop Shadow = Yes

Conclusion

Remember: the sample recommendations above are simply guidelines used successfully for one data system's help system. Your own guidelines may vary, but be sure there are well-thought-out reasons for each guideline decision and that they are thorough in order to render lesson consistency. The more consistent your lessons appear and work, the better they will help the educators who use them. The concept of consistency is developed further in the "Design Consistency" section of this book's "Package/Display Standards: User Interface" chapter.

Data Analysis Lessons

Standard 3.2.01: Present

Offer a comprehensive set of data analysis lessons to cover all common data-related tasks and key data-related topics.

The American Association of School Administrators (AASA) reports teachers know data can help them but are overwhelmed by the data and need help using it (Stansbury, 2013). Most education professionals are not data-savvy and they need help understanding and interpreting data before they can make correctly informed decisions (SAS Institute, 2013). In fact, stakeholders at *all* levels have trouble interpreting data (Underwood et al., 2010). Odendahl (2011) noted that something as complex as test scores cannot be understood without a user's manual.

In addition, most educators analyze data alone for at least part of their data use time, even when there are on-site staff members who could help them on site (USDEOPEPD, 2009). This means that even when staff resources such as data coaches and statisticians are available, educators analyzing a report's data are likely to be doing so without these people's help at times. Other educators simply do not have any on-site data experts assigned to guiding them.

Since most data systems are moving in the direction of being online, educators access and use them outside of the classroom, such as at home in the evening or in a coffee shop on the weekend. It is thus crucial that any data reporting environment include a help system component that serves as a virtual data coach.

A help system should contain lessons that help educators analyze data in the reporting environment. These are the types of lesson most frequently missing from data systems, but they are also the lessons most likely to improve the accuracy of educators' data analyses. Think of the help system's data analysis lessons as a virtual data coach or trainer that can assist educators in appropriately using data when a live person who can help is not present.

Even more so than for the technical lessons, the data analysis lessons in a help system should be written by a data reporting expert who is well versed in region-specific data use. If such an expert cannot be employed at your organization, a team of knowledgeable educators offering to contribute can be enlisted (with gratitude), as long as they all adhere to the same guidelines, particularly those pertaining to lesson consistency (see the Standard 3.1.05 and Standard 3.2.05 sections for consistency details).

Data analysis lessons should be present for all common analysis tasks and key topics. Below is an example of lesson types (e.g., "Data Analysis" manual chapters) appropriate for the data analysis help system component:

- **Definitions** (e.g., Abbreviations, Performance Band, Proficiency Level, Raw Score, Scale Score, Subgroup, etc.);

- **Accountability and Requirements** (e.g., Common Core State Standards FAQ, APR: Understanding API, AYP, PI, etc., AMAOs and Title III Accountability, etc.);

- **Test-Specific** Analyses (e.g., CELDT: Understanding Scores, STAR: Appropriate Grade Level Analysis, STAR: Appropriate Content Cluster Analyses, STAR: Performance Level Cut Points, etc.);

- Popular **Approaches to Data Use** (e.g., Student Grouping, Essential Questions, Data Dialogues, Start of the Year Data Use, Use Data to Differentiate Instruction, etc.);

- Using the System for **Response to Intervention** (RTI) (e.g., Why Use [the Data System] for RTI?, Good Instruction, Regularly Assess Students, Analyze Assessment Results to Determine Student Needs, Tiered Instruction and Intervention, Evaluate RTI Outcomes, Parent Involvement, and Student Involvement);

- **Resources** (Conference Presentations and Handouts, Assessment Design, etc.).

As educators continue to use your data analysis lessons with existing reports, you will identify new needs, or "holes" in the data analysis lesson offering. Respond to these needs with new lessons and/or adjustments to existing lessons.

In addition, you should encourage your clients or colleagues to show users how to access and use the help system and its data analysis lessons. It is likely users will not otherwise know the lessons are there, and most will be grateful for this added resource.

Standard 3.2.02: Accessible

Make lessons: (a) accessible online (e.g., users can share a lesson's URL with other users, Customer Support can share a lesson's URL with a user asking for help, etc.); (b) logically organized so they are easy to manually locate within the help system; (c) searchable (e.g., users can enter a term such as "data dialogues" within the help system and links to relevant lessons will appear); (d) with PDF downloading and printing capabilities; and (e) (in addition to the ever-present help system link) place a specific lesson link/button in each pertinent data system area (e.g., in the part of the system where users customize intervention tiers, offer a link directly to the "Use Intervention Tiers" lesson).

With easy access to data analysis lessons, educators analyzing data "alone" will not be completely alone, as a data expert's guidance will be in the room with them. This expert guidance can support staff in conducting data analyses whenever the educator wants help. Remember: we should not be content to merely give educators data; rather, we should do as much as we can to ensure educators' analyses of that data are *accurate*. The help system's data lessons are crucial to making data reports work for educators.

For a more detailed account of this standard's recommendations, please see Standard 3.1.01 in the "Tech Lessons" section, as the same guidelines apply. In summary, lessons should be:

- **online** (users can share a lesson's URL with other users, just as DSRP Customer Support or District support staff can share a lesson's URL with an educator who calls or emails for help);
- arranged in a **logical** order so it is easy to manually locate a needed lesson within the system;

84

Help System Standards

- **searchable** (educators can enter terms such as "data dialogues" in order for links to relevant lessons to appear);
- **printable** (can be downloaded as PDF files and printed);
- easy to **access** (the help system is one click away via an ever-present Help button, and lessons are well organized within manuals and/or chapters under categories that make sense);
- available via a **link** (suc as a "?" button) within pertinent data system areas (e.g., in the part of the system where users customize intervention tiers, offer a link directly to the "Use Intervention Tiers" lesson).

Standard 3.2.03: Include Lessons for All Users

Include lessons to meet all users' needs, remembering that educators vary greatly in data skills and comfort levels. For example, some users will need introductory lessons with definitions of common terms.

Remember that data users have varied skill levels, and all of these users should be supported in ways well suited to them, just as a good teacher varies his or her instruction for varied students. For example, some users really will need a lesson providing definitions for common abbreviations.

You will need to decide how the help system will be arranged in terms of manuals and chapters so that all users' needs are met and so that all types of user can easily find lessons. In addition to the bulk of your lessons, for which you should try to find middle ground in appealing to as many educators as possible, here are some level-specific ideas:

Novice Users

The number of abbreviations—such as those for demographics, assessments, and accountability—educators must understand is notoriously overwhelming. Many users will thus benefit from an *Abbreviations* lesson that merely provides definitions for these abbreviations. Links to more information on the terms are also helpful.

In addition, it is recommended you provide definitions for educational (e.g., assessment-specific) terms which could confuse some educators, such as a "Definitions" chapter (with lessons like this) or a "Definitions" lesson (with sections like this):

85

Help System Standards

- Performance Band
- Proficiency Level
- Raw Score
- Scale Score
- Subgroup
- and so on.

An added benefit is that whenever you use one of these abbreviations or terms within another lesson, you can feature the word as a link that leads to the definition in the other lesson. This way you will not have to clutter your lesson with added definitions most users will not need, but you will still be supporting users who require explanation.

Some terms will require more than mere definitions. For example, for statistical terms it is helpful to provide examples of their proper application to real-world data use. Thus a "Statistics Basics" chapter could contain lessons like this:

- Generalizability
- Sample Size
- Measurement Error
- Multiple Measures
- and so on.

As with words requiring definitions, whenever you use one of these terms within another lesson, you can feature the term as a link that leads to its term-specific lesson for those who need it.

Advanced Users

If lessons you create specifically for a more data-advanced audience grow to over six, consider creating a separate chapter or manual. These lessons (or a single "Advanced Data Users" link to them) can appear at the bottom of the chapter/manual list so the lessons will not overwhelm or confuse new users.

86

Standard 3.2.04: Key Features

Make lessons: (a) topic-specific (e.g., do not cram a single lesson with everything users might want to do with data), with some task-specific exceptions (e.g., "Use Results to Differentiate Instruction"); (b) region-specific (e.g., as concerns specific assessments and their guidelines); and (c) illustrated (e.g., diagrams, classroom layouts, etc.).

Data analysis help lessons should be:

Topic-Specific

Devote lessons to specific topics (e.g., *State Accountability*). A single lesson should not be crammed with everything anyone might want to understand about data, as that would overwhelm and lose the attention of a large percentage of users.

Note this guideline differs from the help system's tech lessons, which are most frequently task-specific. However, there will also be some task-specific lessons. These typically relate to guidance in specific ways to use data (e.g., "Use Results to Differentiate Instruction"). The need to not cram a single lesson with too much information will become increasingly important as users request more information from their help system over time.

Region-Specific

Lessons should be specific to the client's region (and thus the state assessments being used, graduation and accountability requirements, links for state resources, etc.). This feature is easier to include when only one district or state is using the help system. However, data systems marketed across state lines can provide different help systems (and thus different URL links for the system's "Help" button) customized accordingly.

Illustrated

Include any images (diagrams, graphs, classroom layouts, graphic organizers with links to the actual PDFs, etc.) that will help educators understand and

Help System Standards

Math AYP AMO for Percent of Students (Overall + Each Significant Subgroup) Scoring Proficient or Above

Level	2003–2004	2004–2005	2005–2006	2006–2007	2007–2008	2008–2009	2009–2010	2010–2011	2011–2012	2012–2013	2013–2014
High School & High School District (9–12)	9.6	20.9	20.9	20.9	32.2	43.5	54.8	66.1	77.4	88.7	100
Unified School District, High School District (2–12), & County Office of Education	12.8	23.7	23.7	23.7	34.6	45.5	56.4	67.3	78.2	89.1	100
Elementary School, Middle School, & Elementary School District	16	26.5	26.5	26.5	37	47.5	58	68.5	79	89.5	100

All students as a whole and each subgroup must meet Annual Measurable Objectives (AMOs) that increase each year (as illustrated above) in both ELA and Mathematics.

See the "What Is a Subgroup?" Lesson for details on subgroups.

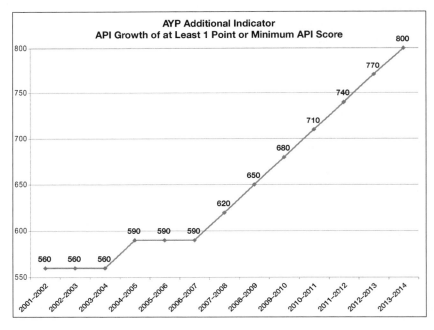

Schools and LEAs must also meet minimum graduation rate requirements (e.g., 90% in 2010), as well as an "additional indicator" tied to API performance, as illustrated above.

Figure 4.3

apply the concept being taught. For example, the table and graph shown in Figure 4.3 were embedded in a lesson helping users to understand their state's accountability requirements.

Standard 3.2.05: Follow Consistency Guidelines

Remain consistent in (a) appearance (e.g., order of info, layout, color choices, etc.) and (b) content type (e.g., users can expect the same types of info from each of the same types of lessons).

Like the help system's tech lessons and other components that help make data easy for educators to use, data analysis lessons should adhere to predetermined guidelines that keep lessons consistent in:

- **appearance** (e.g., layout, order of information, color choices, etc.);
- **content** (e.g., opening lesson description, links for abbreviations and terms, etc.).

Lesson consistency will help users in a number of ways, as outlined earlier for Standard 3.1.05. Thus you and your team (as also described for Standard 3.1.05) will need to decide ahead of time what these consistency guidelines will be. Once established, these guidelines will need to be thoroughly taught to anyone writing lessons for the help system so there is continuity among multiple authors' work. The guidelines you create can be broken sparingly if there is a specific and worthy reason for doing so.

If you have already established consistent guidelines for your tech lessons, you should follow these as closely as possible for each data analysis lesson. I say, "as possible," because the topic-based nature of most of your data analysis lessons (as opposed to the task-based nature of most tech lessons) will mean that some of the guidelines will not apply. For example, a lesson on generalizability will not necessarily feature steps showing where to click in the data system.

If you have not yet established consistent guidelines for your tech lessons, you will find extensive support in the section for Standard 3.1.05. It is best to establish tech lesson guidelines first, as data lessons are not as guideline intensive and can merely follow those tech lesson guidelines that apply.

References

Faria, A., Heppen, J., Li, Y., Stachel, S., Jones, W., Sawyer, K., Palacios, M. et al. (2012, Summer). *Charting success: Data use and student achievement in urban schools*. Council of the Great City Schools and the American Institutes for Research. Retrieved from www.cgcs.org/cms/lib/DC00001581/Centricity/Domain/87/Charting_Success.pdf (accessed October 30, 3015).

Hattie, J. (2010). Visibly learning from reports: The validity of score reports. *Online Educational Research Journal*. Retrieved from www.oerj.org/View?action=view Paper&paper=6 (accessed October 30, 2015).

Kronstadt, J., Moiduddin, A., & Sellheim, W. (2009, March). *Consumer use of computerized applications to address health and health care needs: Prepared for U.S. Department of Health and Human Services, Office of the Secretary, Assistant Secretary for Planning and Evaluation*. Bethesda, MD: NORC at the University of Chicago.

Odendahl, N. V. (2011). *Testwise: Understanding educational assessment, Volume 1*. Lanham, MD: Rowman & Littlefield Education.

O'Hanlon, L. H. (2013, March 14). Designing better PD models. *Education Week*, 32(25), 16–17.

Papay, J., Harvard Graduate School of Education (2007). *Aspen Institute datasheet: The teaching workforce*. Washington, DC: The Aspen Institute.

Piehler, C. (2014, March 10). Survey finds 50 percent of K-12 teachers get inadequate support for using technology in the classroom. *THE Journal*. Retrieved from https://thejournal.com/articles/2014/03/10/digedu-survey-results.aspx (accessed October 30, 2015).

SAS Institute (2013). *Best practices in information management, reporting and analytics for education*. Retrieved from https://fs24.formsite.com/edweek/form15/secure_index.html (accessed October 30, 2015).

Stansbury, M. (2013, July). Nine templates to help educators leverage school data: New industry collaborative says using data effectively can help close education gaps. *eSchool News*. Retrieved from www.eschoolnews.com/2013/01/07/nine-templates-to-help-educators-leverage-school-data/?ast=104&astc=9990 (accessed May 25, 2015)

Underwood, J. S., Zapata-Rivera, D., & VanWinkle, W. (2010). An evidence-centered approach to using assessment data for policymakers. *ETS Research Rep. RR-10-03*. Princeton, NJ: ETS.

U.S. Department of Education Office of Planning, Evaluation and Policy Development (2009). *Implementing data-informed decision making in schools: Teacher access, supports and use*. United States Department of Education (ERIC Document Reproduction Service No. ED504191).

Van der Meij, H. (2008). Designing for user cognition and affect in a manual. Should there be special support for the latter? *Learning and Instruction*, 18(1), 18–29.

5 | Package/Display Standards
Big Picture

Definition of Package/Display

The way in which a data system and its reports are packaged or displayed relates to the tool's design, such as its data visualization, user interface, and more. Data that is "over-the-counter" is presented to users with package/display that renders easy and accurate use of data system/report content. Effective package/display:

- maintains **credibility** through secure, error-free data and displays;
- contains **key features** such as summaries and calculations, vital data, appropriate graphs, and clear headers;
- employs effective **design** practices;
- offers efficient **navigation**;
- provides useful **input controls** (shown here), which allow users to customize reports.

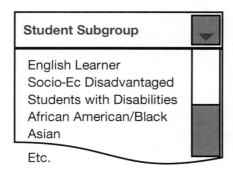

Figure 5.1

Package/Display Standards: Big Picture

Improved package/display within a data system and its reports contributes to easier data system use, easier data use, and more accurate data use.

Consider over-the-counter products again. Educators should never consume medicine packaged in a way that lacks credibility (e.g., the label contains spelling errors) or features poor design (e.g., the box shows childlike images implying the medicine is for children when it is actually only for adults). Likewise, educators should never be expected to consume data that is poorly packaged and displayed. In both cases, correct use impacts lives. Thus design should actively encourage appropriate use.

How to Implement Package/Display Standards

Resources

Access the following:

- OTCD *Package/Display* standards (on pages 6–11 of OTCD Standards)
- Details on research-based evidence supporting OTCD *Package/ Display* standards

An ideal data reporting environment should reflect the OTCD *Package/ Display* standards, which stipulate research-based ways data systems/reports can be designed effectively. These standards can be found online with details on the extensive research informing every standard. The rest of this chapter contains a lesson on how to implement each OTCD *Package/ Display* standard.

Package/Display Standards: Big Picture

Real-World Implementation: Package/Display

By Rudi Lewis, Chief Operating Officer, Silverback Learning Solutions

The core feature set that went into Silverback Mileposts was built out of sheer necessity by educators who needed a better way. They wanted to optimize learning for every student, without letting one student fall through the cracks, by equipping teachers with tools to have an easy-to-update portfolio for every child, and use data as a wellness exam, not an autopsy. But how do you infuse the voice of the educator without fostering an anything-goes, customer-compelled Frankenstein of a product? Good design is paramount to this process.

First, we foster input from teachers, administrators, and our own staff through a one-click feature request button in our help menu and an annual conference. We synthesize ideas down by grouping similar requests, then we estimate the engineering time and rank the request with all others on the roadmap. This helps inform our design of the report suite and other system features in a way that incorporates user feedback without sacrificing the long-range vision.

Navigation and input controls have to be easy and fast. Take the most-used path from your customer walkthroughs, and make sure you've got teachers there in fewer than three clicks. Also, let teachers "shift gears" quickly and easily, from adding new slices of data to reports, to shifting between reports and visualizations. Don't make teachers climb all the way back down the stairs every time they want to grab a quick piece of data from the cellar.

No matter how cool your interface is, don't overlook data accuracy. Your credibility and your relationship with your customer depend on it. This is as much a service commitment as it is an engineering commitment. Repeatedly, districts turned to our company because the data in our reports was correct, timely, and came with our guarantee to be responsive if it wasn't.

And of course: design with security as a core feature, not an afterthought. Think how a parent would think—make the data theirs and present it to them in ways that deliver useful information on how their children are learning, and they'll have a much easier time understanding why this same data is useful in the hands of their children's teachers. In October 2014, The Future of Privacy Forum (FPF) and the Software & Information Industry Association (SIIA) announced a K-12 school service providers Pledge to safeguard student privacy built around a dozen commitments regarding the collection, maintenance, and use of students' personal information. Make sure this Pledge is part of your design rules and you'll create a system that parents can support with confidence—you'll need parents to support your system and your cause if you truly believe you can help drive better achievement for all kids.

Credibility

Standard 4.1.01: No Wrong Data

Safeguard against displaying incorrect data. For example, ensure: (a) reports work properly (e.g., do not "duplicate-count" or erroneously convert a numeric score to a percentage); (b) reports pull data from the right places; and (c) original data files are as appropriately formatted, clean/correct, and complete as possible.

Data visualization expert Edward Tufte (2011) said the most important task of someone presenting data is to establish and keep credibility. Credibility means the data can be trusted (its source, its accuracy, etc.).

You would not use an over-the-counter product if its box was torn open, the bottle inside had a broken seal, or its label was fraught with spelling errors. This is because a product's credibility and safety impact someone's ability to use and benefit from that product.

To have good over-the-counter data (OTCD) that is thus easy for educators to use—just as with good over-the-counter medicine—the way in which data is packaged or displayed must establish and maintain credibility.

The fastest killer of a data system's credibility is wrong data. **Examples:**

- If a user knows a school site has about 20 English Learner (EL) students, but a data system report indicates there are *375* EL students at the site, that is wrong data.

Package/Display Standards: Big Picture

- If a user pulls up two reports that both include 7th graders' performance on a specific test in a specific year, and one report says 58 percent scored *Proficient* while another report says *81 percent* scored *Proficient*, at least one of the reports is displaying wrong data.

- If a user sees a report claiming, *"285%* of your female students are expected to graduate on time," he or she is looking at wrong data (or possibly an unnecessary percent sign).

Some errors might be due to problems with data that districts are providing to the DSRP (which should then be rectified by educators with any needed DSRP support), but others might be due to problems with the way the reports were built. Every data file in a data system typically has some degree of error, but any underlying structural or programming errors should be identified and corrected, or else the data cannot be considered reliable (U.S. Government Accountability Office, 2009).

Wrong data means educators cannot trust a report, and this could lead to not trusting the data system. When rolling out a new data report, work closely with key stakeholders to see if any of the numbers look suspicious. While the report might look functional on your end, its users will better know whether the displayed data is accurate.

When users report problems with displayed data, garner specifics from them concerning what is wrong. See the "Work with Educators" chapter in this book for support in acquiring troubleshooting information you need.

With the educator's help, you can ensure:

- reports work properly (e.g., do not duplicate-count, which means counting the same piece of data twice, as when a student is in more than one English class and is then wrongly counted twice in a summary of the English Department's performance; do not erroneously convert a numeric score to a percent, etc.);

- reports pull data from the right places.

You might need to work with a district's IT Department, which can ensure that original data files are as appropriately formatted, clean/correct, and complete as possible.

The root cause of wrong data should be uncovered, and educators can be a tremendous help with this. For example, since the DSRP is far removed from the students, the DSRP will not necessarily know at a glance that a number is clearly "off" in the way an educator often will. District administrators and site office staff can be especially helpful in this respect (e.g., How many GATE students do we have? How many students in the SDC classes do we have? etc.). DSRPs and educators can work together to get this problem remedied if it is found.

Based on what is determined to be the problem and how the system's data tables are structured, DSRPs and educators should also double-check any other reports that might have a similar problem to the one that was found. In some cases, fixing the data problem for one report also solves it for other reports, but this is often not the case.

Standard 4.1.02: No Inappropriate Displays or Calculations

When determining how to display data and how to calculate values: (a) adhere to guidelines specific to the data being displayed (e.g., don't show accountability scores over time on a line graph, implying growth, if those particular accountability scores cannot be used to determine growth) or calculated (e.g., do not subtract one grade level's test score from another's and emphasize the difference if that particular test is not scaled across grade levels); (b) select displays and calculations most likely to encourage correct analyses of the particular data being displayed; and (c) do not simplify the data presentation to the point that misunderstandings are likely.

We want data to be simple, but sometimes the simplest displays are not accurate. This is one of the reasons why having programmers build whatever educators ask for (without an overseeing DSRP reporting expert) is dangerous. The report format that users prefer can be the opposite of the report format through which people most accurately interpret and most appropriately use data (Hattie, 2010).

For example, for many standardized exams you cannot subtract one year's test score from the next and call it growth, because those particular tests vary in difficulty from one year to the next. Educators still frequently ask for such a comparison for these particular exams, whereas there are better ways to show growth for those particular assessments.

Package/Display Standards: Big Picture

If your reports ignore recommended approaches to displays of particular data, this risks credibility. Worse, doing so can mislead educators and hurt students.

 Common examples of the types of mistakes data systems and reports are prone to making (and thus mistakes to watch out for) are featured in the "Common Inappropriate Data Displays" table. To demonstrate how common these pitfalls are, California's Standardized Testing and Reporting (STAR) tests used for state testing prior to Common Core State Standards (CCSS), Academic Performance Index (API) used for state accountability, and Adequate Yearly Progress (AYP) used (like other states) for federal accountability, comprised a data collection that exemplified *all* of the criteria to look out for in the table's "If This Is True of Your Data" column.

Since some data systems and reports (and some educators) overlook the analysis guidelines that accompany such assessments and accountability systems, this means the educators using these tools are at risk of using inappropriate calculations and displays to analyze their data. Perhaps the scariest aspect of this problem is that educators are often using the reports without knowing the analyses that the report formats encourage are flawed.

Another common inappropriate display or calculation, which is not exclusive to performance data, relates to comparing counts from separate entities rather than percentages when those entities differ in total number

Example: If a report suggests, "Teacher A had 32 students score proficient, whereas Teacher B only had 28 students score proficient," this can be misleading if Teacher A had 38 students in class (obtaining 84 percent proficiency) while Teacher B had only 28 students in class (obtaining 100 percent proficiency). Percentages are almost always more favorable to numbers when reporting on performance because they allow multiple entities to be more easily (and more appropriately) compared. Numbers are more helpful when a report will be used for logistics, such as grouping students in a class, scheduling students at a school site, ordering materials for students in a district, etc. When less important, counts can be featured in smaller fonts to communicate their reduced importance while still making them available (such as to support users considering sample size).

(Jones, 2007; Underwood, 2013). This might apply to comparing different class periods, different grade levels, etc. See the example on page 97.

Educators and DSRP reporting experts who understand each region-specific data source's analysis intricacies and limitations (e.g., ways in which data from a particular exam should—vs. should not—be calculated, displayed, or used) are often the only ones aware of whether or not a data display is inappropriate. These people should check data system displays and reports to be sure none are misleading and no problems exist in the way data is displayed. For example, you should make sure data displays and value calculations:

- adhere to guidelines specific to the data being displayed (e.g., do not show accountability scores over time on a line graph, implying growth, if those particular accountability scores cannot be used to determine growth);
- adhere to guidelines specific to the data being calculated (e.g., do not subtract one grade level's test score from another's and emphasize the difference if that particular test is not scaled across grade levels);
- are used based on those most likely to encourage correct analyses of the particular data being displayed;
- do not simplify the data presentation to the point that misunderstandings are likely.

Standard 4.1.03: No Sloppiness

Ensure the data system and its reports contain no: (a) misspellings; (b) errors in grammar or capitalization (including tags for case-sensitive searching); (c) unintentional font changes (in type, style, or size); (d) cut-off text (e.g., due to cell or page limitations); (e) sloppy formatting (lines missing or overlapping, inconsistent spacing between graphs, varied row height for no reason, etc.); or (f) inflexibility to variations (e.g., graph bar colors do not adhere to intended colors/meanings if an assessment has fewer proficiency levels than usual).

Remember the example given earlier about reading a medication label fraught with spelling errors. If the maker could not spend five minutes using spellcheck, how likely is the maker to have invested adequate time and energy into ensuring the product contents are safe, reliable, and effective? The same question gets posed by educators encountering sloppiness in a data system or report, and the answer to the question is equally grim.

A Stanford University study involving 2,684 participants found the visual design of a site (e.g., typography, layout, font size, etc.) was mentioned most frequently (in 46.1 percent of comments) when evaluating a website's credibility (Fogg et al., 2002). Aspects such as those described below can have a highly significant impact on users' trust in a web-based data system or the reports it generates.

No Misspellings

Verbiage within the data system and/or individual reports should feature no misspellings. If you utilize reporting software that does not offer spellcheck, the text can still be pasted into another format (e.g., Microsoft Word) to quickly check it for errors. Use spellcheck with a discriminating eye (e.g., spellcheck is not always familiar with terms used only in education).

Proper Grammar and Capitalization

Verbiage within the data system and/or individual reports should feature correct grammar and capitalization. Note automated error checks might not correctly manage terms and abbreviations specific to education. Capitalization errors can also interfere with report searches (e.g., when a report is tagged as "ayp" rather than the "AYP" by which Adequate Yearly Progress is properly abbreviated, and a data system's method of searching for reports is case specific, any searches for "AYP" would fail to find the report).

No Unintentional Font Changes

This includes changes in:

- font type (e.g., the report is in Arial but one cell is in Times New Roman),
- style (e.g., changing from bold to italics for no reason), and
- size (e.g., the report is in 10pt but one cell is in 8pt without good reason).

Package/Display Standards: Big Picture

There should be no unintentional font changes within a data system and/or its reports.

> See **Examples** C and D in the next chapter (in color online). Example C (Before) had an unintentional font change in font type and size on its bottom row. The font was corrected in Example D (After).

No Cut-Off Text

Text should never cut off prematurely. This problem can happen due to cell or page limitations or due to poorly placed images or graphics.

If your report is generated within a data system where users can customize the report via input controls, run the report with varied input controls (e.g., be sure a long school or student name can fit in its assigned location) to be sure this is not a problem.

> See **Examples** C and D again. Example C (Before) cut off the ending text on its header. The text problem was corrected in Example D (After).

No Sloppy Formatting

Reports should not feature problems like this:

- Lines are missing.
- Text, lines, or images overlap where they should not.
- The spacing between graphs is not consistent (for no good reason).
- Rows differ in height (for no good reason).
- The established color/coding system is violated (e.g., when a score is in the *Proficient* range its cell is colored green, yet in some areas these scores' cells accidentally remain red).

Package/Display Standards: Big Picture

Flexible to Variations

If a report is generated within a data system where users can customize it via input controls, be sure some control selections will not result in problems.

> **Example:** Bar colors on a graph look great, ranging from red for the lowest of five proficiency levels to green for the highest, when the report is generated for a test with five levels of proficiency. However, when the report is run for an assessment with four or fewer proficiency levels it throws all the colors off.

Conclusion

If a DSRP cannot spend five minutes cleaning up an accidental change in font size or type, text getting cut off, or cell formatting that was overlooked, how can educators trust the accuracy of the data it displays? The truth is they cannot.

Standard 4.1.04: Private and Secure

Conform to best practices and legislation for data privacy and security.

Educators are responsible for data governance and ensuring data is properly collected, inputted, and maintained. Keeping data private and secure is required at each of these stages in the data's journey, and this means any data system educators use must be designed to keep its data content private and secure.

For example, data systems should make it easy for users to:

- keep data private so only those with the right to see particular data can see it (e.g., users have individualized access to student data that can be controlled by a district administrator with supervisorial access);

- keep data secure (e.g., user-specific passwords and a hack-proof system);

- conform to related regulations, such as the Family Educational Rights and Privacy Act (FERPA), which impacts many school districts.

The technical requirements for effective data protection are ever-evolving, as hackers continually find new ways to compromise data systems, and the technology used to compromise or protect data changes rapidly. Resources that can help DSRPs remain up to date with changing needs include:

- Data Quality Campaign (*www.dataqualitycampaign.org/*);
- Software and Information Industry Association (SIIA) and the Future of Privacy Forum (FPF) Student Privacy Pledge (*http://studentprivacy pledge.org/*);
- The State Educational Technology Directors Association (SETDA) (*www.setda.org/*);
- The U.S. Department of Education's Family Policy Compliance Office (FPCO) (*www2.ed.gov/policy/gen/guid/fpco/index.html*);
- The U.S. Department of Education's Privacy Technical Assistance Center (PTAC) (*http://ptac.ed.gov*).

References

Fogg, B. J., Soohoo, C., Danielson, D., Marable, L., Stanford, J., & Tauber, E. (2002, October 29). *How do people evaluate a web site's credibility? Results from a large study.* Retrieved from www.consumerwebwatch.org/pdfs/stanfordPTL.pdf (no longer available).

Hattie, J. (2010). Visibly learning from reports: The validity of score reports. *Online Educational Research Journal.* Retrieved from www.oerj.org/View?action= viewPaper&paper=6 (accessed October 30, 2015).

Jones, G. E. (2007). *How to lie with charts* (2nd ed.). Santa Monica, CA: LaPuerta.

Tufte, E. (2011, December 8) *Presenting data and information.* Presentation conducted from the Westin San Francisco Market Street, San Francisco, CA.

Underwood, J. (2013). *Data visualization best practices.* Retrieved from www.slide share.net/idigdata/data-visualization-best-practices-2013 (accessed October 30, 2015).

U.S. Government Accountability Office (2009, July). *Assessing the reliability of computer-processed data, external version I, report #GAO-09-680G.* Washington, DC: Author.

Package/Display Standards

Report Design

Report Design Aspects

The last chapter covered the introduction to the *Package/Display* standards and "big picture" concerns such as credibility, which involves the data reports themselves but also outside factors such as loading data files. This chapter zeroes in on data reports and how their data is packaged or displayed for users. It covers two related aspects: key features and design.

Adding key features to reports and using research-based design conventions helps educators understand the report's data as quickly and easily as possible. The time one person/programmer spends adding and/or improving key features within a report or improving the report's design is miniscule compared to the time it will collectively save the many educators using the report. More importantly, the successful incorporation of key features and effective design will significantly reduce chances of the report's data being misunderstood, misused, and/or not used at all.

Key Features

Standard 4.2.01: Summaries/Averages for Comparison

Include the summaries/averages that will best provide context for the types of comparisons users will want to make when they use the report (this requires understanding the report's purpose and use). For example, a class list of 35 students' scores will likely require a "Class" row averaging each column's data.

Most data means nothing without a point of comparison. The National Association of States Boards of Education (2012) cited one of the four key ways data needs to be communicated in a way useful to answering critical questions as that it be contextual, allowing for comparisons of data to that of larger entities such as school or district in order to compare trends. The American Educational Research Association (AERA) recommended summaries of rows and columns as vital comparison points for other data in the table, with the type of summary (e.g., sum, average, or median) chosen based on purpose (Wainer, 1992).

> **Example:** Imagine I am a teacher at a school with optimum data transparency, and I am looking at a list of 20 teachers showing how each teacher's students averaged on a test. If I find my own row of data on that list, how do I instantly know how my students performed in relation to my colleagues' students? The table should contain an average for the whole site or department to which I can compare my row's numbers.

Displayed comparisons give data added meaning, and you should not have to run a separate report to make a likely comparison. Likewise, displayed comparisons help prevent educators from running mental calculations (covered for Standard 4.2.02).

Typically, a list of students in a class should feature an average for the whole class, a list of school sites should feature an average for the whole district if other sites have the same data, etc. However, summaries/averages can also encapsulate other data, such as in the upcoming examples.

Reports should include the summaries/averages that will best support the types of comparisons that will give the data meaning and that educators will want to make when they use the report. This is one of many reasons why a report's purpose should be closely considered when the report is designed.

Package/Display Standards: Report Design

See **Examples** A and B in this chapter (in color online). Example B (After) features a row at the bottom with averages not only for the group of students on the table, but also for the whole school and district, to which each student and the group as a whole can now be compared. Thus educators instantly see if their own students' strengths/weaknesses differ from these larger groups'.

Also, Example A (Before) forced users to look at many cells for each student to determine if each student is *Proficient*. Example B (After) displays this proficiency determination at the end of each student's row, making it clear while also allowing differences from one year to the next to jump out. The graphs also support easy comparison.

Note how each key feature shown in the *After* version helps users understand and use the data:

- **Summaries/averages** are displayed to provide context and allow for comparison.

- **Calculations** are displayed for the user, as any mental calculation poses some risk in accuracy.

- **Vital data** is included in the report.

- **Graphs** are used for key information and are used well (e.g., they are not 3-dimensional, since 2-dimensional graphs are less likely to distort the viewer's understanding of actual values).

- **Clear headers** provide added information and distinguish between data types.

See **Examples** C and D again. Example D (After) features a row at the bottom with averages and totals to which each site can now be compared. The added information at the bottom lets users know how school sites performed in relation to the district as a whole, and users can quickly see each site's ultimate proficiency achievement. In Example C (Before), this achievement was only available broken out into two separate columns (*Proficient* and *Advanced*), and their values needed to be mentally added together to know how many students, together, achieved proficiency.

Student	Grade	US School Entry	CELDT Prof Level Listening 2008–2009	CELDT Prof Level Listening 2009–2010	CELDT Prof Level Listening Growth	CELDT Prof Level Speaking 2008–2009	CELDT Prof Level Speaking 2009–2010	CELDT Prof Level Speaking Growth	CELDT Prof Level Reading 2008–2009	CELDT Prof Level Reading 2009–2010	CELDT Prof Level Reading Growth	CELDT Prof Level Writing 2008–2009	CELDT Prof Level Writing 2009–2010	CELDT Prof Level Writing Growth	CELDT Prof Level Overall 2008–2009	CELDT Prof Level Overall 2009–2010	CELDT Prof Level Overall Growth
Dees, Alotta	7	09/01/06	2.0	3.0	1.0	2.0	2.0	0.0	2.0	3.0	1.0	2.0	3.0	1.0	2.0	2.8	0.8
Learn, Wanda	7	12/02/07	3.0	4.0	1.0	3.0	3.0	0.0	4.0	4.0	0.0	1.0	3.0	2.0	2.8	3.5	0.8
Lerner, Earl E.	8	03/04/08	4.0	5.0	1.0	3.0	4.0	1.0	5.0	4.0	-1.0	2.0	3.0	0.0	3.5	3.8	0.3
Reed, Khan	7	02/09/08	5.0	4.0	-1.0	4.0	5.0	1.0	5.0	3.0	-2.0	3.0	4.0	1.0	4.3	4.0	-0.3
Taker, Tess	7	01/17/08	3.0	2.0	-1.0	2.0	3.0	1.0	2.0	2.0	0.0	1.0	2.0	1.0	2.0	2.3	0.3
Turner, Paige	8	11/16/08	3.0	4.0	1.0	1.0	3.0	2.0	4.0	4.0	0.0	2.0	4.0	2.0	2.5	3.8	1.3
Wright, Mark	7	12/20/05	2.0	3.0	1.0	3.0	4.0	1.0	3.0	4.0	1.0	2.0	3.0	1.0	2.5	3.5	1.0
Average	N/A	N/A	3.1	3.6	0.4	2.6	3.4	0.9	3.6	3.4	-0.1	1.9	3.0	1.1	2.8	3.4	0.6

Figure 6.1 Example A (Before)

- No labels (missing title and footer).
- Missing important summaries and calculations, as well as vital data (e.g., School and District averages).
- Missing graphs and clear headers.
- Too much clutter due to unnecessary lines and poor formatting.
- Missing purposeful color and shading.
- Size of text does not reflect its importance.

English Language Proficiency Growth

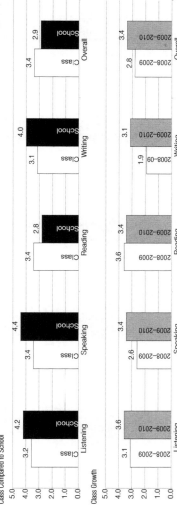

Figure 6.2 Example B (After)

- All problems noted in the *Before* example have been solved.
- Key user questions are now answered by the calculations in the last two columns, clear headers in the top three rows, vital data on the whole school's performance, summaries/averages in the last three table rows, and graphs at the bottom.

Package/Display Standards: Report Design

Standard 4.2.02: Calculations Done for You

Provide calculations that prevent users from having to perform mental arithmetic when analyzing data (e.g., if displaying performance over multiple years on a vertically scaled assessment, display any appropriate, relevant growth calculations). Note calculations can also result in words rather than numbers, such as a proficiency determination.

Educators should not have to perform mental arithmetic when analyzing data. Rather, data reports should include necessary calculations directly within the reports, as even those who understand the data and know which calculations to make can make math mistakes when forced to perform mental arithmetic (The National Research Council [NRC], 2001).

For example:

- If proficiency levels are broken down (35 percent of students are *Proficient* and 24 percent are *Advanced*, meaning 59 percent of students met proficiency standards), these added sums should also be displayed for educators on the report.

- If you are looking at performance over multiple years, you should see the growth or change calculated in its own row or column.

Research indicates missing sums and averages can:

- discourage staff from using a report;
- open staff's analyses up to error; or
- open staff's use of the data up to error.

Any time educators are expected to perform mental arithmetic when using a report, there is a risk of error.

Consider the "before" and "after" versions of a report's table on the next page (in color online). Notice how the table is improved by the inclusion of calculations the report's users likely need, as well as by adhering to other OTCD Standards.

Calculations can also result in words rather than numbers. For example, educators might have to add up or consider multiple scores to determine whether or not a student is considered *At Risk* or *Proficient*, and the report should not force them to take such steps. Just like numerical sums, such determinations should be displayed clearly for users. See the description of examples on page 110.

108

Package/Display Standards: Report Design

Percent (and Number) of Students Earning Each Performance Level on the English Language Arts California Standards Test					
Sites	Far Below Basic	Below Basic	Basic	Proficient	Advanced
Ames High School	4% (10)	9% (23)	29% (73)	35% (89)	24% (61)
Anita Book Inter. School	6% (12)	7% (16)	26% (56)	43% (93)	17% (37)
Chance Continuation School	19% (21)	27% (30)	38% (42)	14% (16)	2% (2)
Earl E. Lerner Elem. School	4% (8)	15% (34)	30% (68)	32% (71)	19% (43)

Figure 6.3 Example C (Before)

- Cut-off text, unintentional font changes, and other formatting errors.
- Missing important summaries and calculations, as well as clear headers.
- The reader's eye cannot easily compare values due to clutter, line-hugging, and poor formatting.
- Size of text does not reflect its importance.

% and # of Students Earning Each Performance Level (PL) on ELA CST						
Sites	Far Below Basic	Below Basic	Basic	Proficient	Advanced	Proficiency Achieved (Sum of 2 Highest PLs)
Ames High School 256 students	4% 10	9% 23	29% 73	35% 89	24% 61	59% 150
Anita Book Inter. School 214 students	6% 12	7% 16	26% 56	43% 93	17% 37	61% 130
Chance Continuation School 111 students	19% 21	27% 30	38% 42	14% 16	2% 2	16% 18
Earl E. Lerner Elem. School 224 students	4% 8	15% 34	30% 68	32% 71	19% 43	51% 114
Average Performance 805 students	8% 51	15% 103	31% 239	31% 269	16% 143	47% 412

Figure 6.4 Example D (After)

- All the problems noted in the *Before* example have been solved:

Package/Display Standards: Report Design

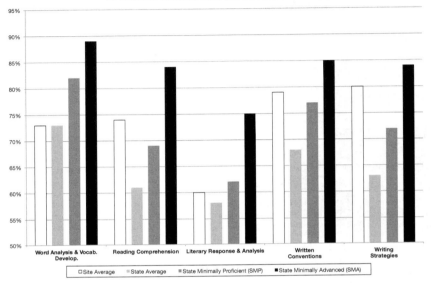

Figure 6.5 Example E (Before)

- Inefficient labels (the title belies how complicated this data is to understand, and a footer is missing)
- Missing important calculations and vital data needed for correct analyses
- Graph and format are inappropriate for this particular assessment's data, which requires State Minimally Proficient (SMP) scores to be compared to Site scores to judge performance
- Contributes to clutter with unnecessary lines
- Uses a key/legend rather than displaying entities
- Size of text does not reflect its importance

> - See **Examples** A and B again. Example A (Before) forced users to consider multiple columns of data to determine each student's proficiency status. Two slim columns in Example B (After) save users from having to consider data in 70 different cells just to determine seven students' proficiency statuses for each of two years.

110

Package/Display Standards: Report Design

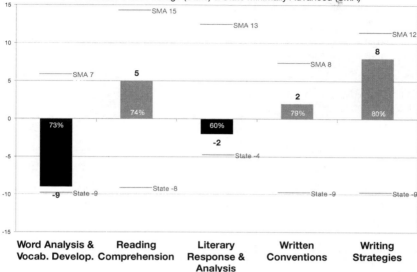

Figure 6.6 Example F (After)

- All problems noted in the *Before* example have been solved.
- Even though *After* might look harder to understand than *Before*, it is actually easier for the educator to make *correct* analyses because:
  - To garner value from the data in *Before*, educators had to subtract each score for State Minimally Proficient (SMP)—or (though less reliable due to smaller sample size) the State Minimally Advanced (SMA)—from each score for Site. Since the sum of those calculations is what suggests possible strengths/weaknesses, *After* graphs that (most important) data for the user.
  - Note all other values from *Before* are still featured in *After*, along with the new (and more important) values as points of comparison, but they are graphed less obtrusively since they are less important.
  - Even if the user does not spend more than five seconds trying to understand *After*, he or she can instantly guess which of Site's scores are worse (red, lower/negative numbers) and which are better (green, higher/positive numbers).

> ● See **Examples** E and F in this chapter (in color online). If an educator viewing Example E (Before) did know the site's cluster scores only have meaning as compared to the State Minimally Proficient (SMP) or State Minimally Advanced (SMA) for this particular assessment, he or she would still have to subtract each cluster's SMP percent from the Site percent and then compare those numbers to each other. Example F (After) provides those totals for the educator and graphs them.

Reports should include calculations that will best give the data meaning and that will prevent educators from having to perform arithmetic in their heads. This arithmetic extends to considering multiple datasets to make determinations such as whether or not a student is considered *Proficient.*

Standard 4.2.03: Vital Data Included

Display all data required for a report to function most effectively. Do not require users to look elsewhere to acquire data a user needs (a) to properly use the report or (b) for the report to achieve its intended purpose (e.g., if users must hover or click to "drill down" to added info, that added info must not be essential to the report's primary purpose).

We all want data to be simple, but sometimes it is not. Educators sometimes prefer data reports that turn out to be less effective in rendering accurate analyses (Hattie, 2010). For example, graphs like the one used as an example in the "Label Standards" chapter of this book often contain only the data bars pertaining to the district's performance. While the way in which the graph example is structured is flawed to begin with, it is the most common format used by data systems and often omits the vital SMP data bars, rendering the rest of that particular assessment report's data meaningless. In that case, reports without the added data look easier to use, but they are useless (and misleading) without the vital state data.

As another example, early warning system reports (often included in data systems) are used to identify students "at risk" in some way, such as for not graduating or not being ready for college. Since multiple factors

Package/Display Standards: Report Design

can contribute to risk status, these factors are often scaled, weighted, and/or aggregated into a single score. Displaying such a score on reports is helpful, but some systems display *only* this score on reports, making the user click each student's record to drill down to the data that contributed to his or her final score.

Such a simplified report defeats the report's purpose. The whole reason an educator would view the report would be to inform an action (e.g., to know an "at risk" student's particular weak areas so the educator can offer help in those areas, or to know where a site's students are struggling most so programs, interventions, or improved absence processes can be offered to target that particular area).

A report's user should not have to look elsewhere (e.g., drill down) in various places to learn what the report should be expected to display. Educators should be given all the data they need to properly use a report and achieve the report's purpose. Drilling down to additional data works best for *ancillary* tasks.

Examples of reports improved by the inclusion of vital data include:

- See **Examples** A and B again. Example A (Before) showed averages for the group featured on the table, but there was nothing to which educators could compare this group (e.g., if the table was run for students in an intervention program, how did they compare to the school as a whole?). Example B (After) features bottom rows with averages for the whole school and district, to which each student and the group as a whole can now be compared. Thus educators can instantly see if their own students' strengths/ weaknesses differ from these larger groups'.

- See **Examples** E and F again. By leaving the actual data off the graph, Example E (Before) makes comparisons much harder to conduct. Even though the graph is consolidated in Example F (After), the actual number that matters for every bar on the Before graph is included on the After graph, so no vital data is missing.

Package/Display Standards: Report Design

Standard 4.2.04: Graph as Appropriate

Include graph(s) when appropriate while adhering to graph guidelines such as: (a) use graphs only for key info/comparisons (e.g., use graphs to point out important occurrences—such as trends—that are easily missed in a table, but do not graph all available data); (b) select graph type based on ease of use and its suitability to the graph's purpose; (c) include 0 on the scale of an axis (rather than narrowing its displayed range) and make the scale read from left to right (e.g., scales on a horizontal, such as a table's row of column headers, should begin with the lowest value in the leftmost location and end with the highest value in the rightmost location); (d) use 2-dimensional (not 3-D) graphs; (e) place data directly on the graph (e.g., if a bar represents 36 percent of students, display "36%" above the bar); and (f) consider # of entities (e.g., if 78 schools would each appear as bars on a graph, rendering the graph cluttered and ineffective, default to a modified display).

Have you ever heard someone say, "I am not a visual learner"? It is rare for someone to feel this way, regardless of controversy surrounding the merit of learning styles. There is extensive research supporting the use of graphs in reports. When viewing the research information eResource, note the relative consistency among evidence, even over time.

Reports should not only include a graph when appropriate; they should also adhere to research-based graph guidelines to increase each report's effectiveness. Key guidelines are:

Only for Key Info/Comparisons

Using a graphic for everything defeats the purpose. Charts or graphs should be included for key comparisons and to point out important occurrences— such as trends—that might be easily missed in a tabular format.

Do not let the benefits of graphs make you feel graphs are always superior to tables and other displays. There is still value in tabular format, so use tables when appropriate. In fact, using a combination of approaches helps key comparisons and information garner notice. Otherwise, pages and pages of graphs can become as overwhelming and ineffective as pages and pages of tabled data.

114

See **Examples** A and B again. When the content from Example A (Before) was used to create the improved Example B (After), graphs were added to highlight key points. All report information could have been graphed, but that would be overload. Instead, two graphs in Example B (After) address the two biggest topics users would likely want to explore with this report, and the graphs' implications pop out.

Best Graph = Easy + Appropriate

Select graph type based on ease of use and its suitability to the graph's purpose. Helpful resources (e.g., what to use a histogram for) include: Alverson (2008); Aschbacher and Herman (1991); Bernhardt (2004); Clark and Lyons (2004); Data Quality Campaign (2010); Goodman and Hambleton (2004); Kosslyn (2006); National Research Council (2001); and Sabbah (2011).

0 on Scale/Left

Include 0 on the scale. While it is tempting to narrow an axis's range to make graph bar or line differences easier to spot, this can misrepresent values and make multiple graphs of different entities harder to compare accurately (e.g., when comparing the same test score graph generated for different students).

If you must narrow an axis's range (e.g., accountability scores on a 1–1,000 scale always land between 850 and 1,000 because a score under 850 is impossible, and all scores look the same when graphed unless the axis range is narrowed to 850–1,000), do so with reservation, knowing the possible repercussions. Using the correct scale will show data more accurately and consistently (Bernhardt, 2004).

In addition, scales should read from left to right. Most users read left to right (as with English) and not right to left (as with Hebrew). Scales on a horizontal (such as a table's row of column headers) should begin with the lowest values in the leftmost scale locations and end with the highest values in the rightmost locations. Eyetrack observations found the eye typically begins at the top left corner of a webpage or image, which is the eye's most comfortable starting position, and then moves just as most cultures read: from left to right and then top to bottom, even to the point where the leftmost words in a headline are as important as the placement of the headline (Outing & Ruel, 2006). Jones (2007) writes that appropriate charts do not feature reversed scales, and Underwood (2013) notes reversing scales is a common problem with poor data visualization.

No 3-D

Use two-dimensional (not three-dimensional) graphs. Despite a 3-D graphing trend that surged in the 1980s under the assumption that 3-D images look cool and/or high-tech, research over time has remained consistent that 3-D graphs are not preferred by education stakeholders (Sabbah, 2011). Three-dimensional graphs can make hard-to-understand information harder to grasp (Bernhardt, 2004) and can cause problems with size judgments (NRC, 2001; Tufte, 2011).

Data Directly on Graph

Graphs should display the actual data (i.e., include numbers and percentages on the graph) (Tufte, 2011). For example, if a bar on a graph represents 82 percent of students, then "82%" should actually be displayed directly above that bar. While you might fear this adds clutter, it is the valuable kind of clutter that prevents the educator from having to look somewhere else to find specific data that should be readily available. One purpose of eliminating bad clutter is so you can include more of the kind of information that helps.

Consider # of Entities

Another kind of clutter happens when you graph too many entities. For example, a line graph might look great if it tracks the progress of three types of student (Limited English Proficient vs. English Only vs. Redesignated Fluent English Proficient), but if you use the same graph to track the progress of every demographic of student the graph becomes too hard to

Package/Display Standards: Report Design

read and thus useless. This is a particularly critical consideration for line graphs, which are great for showing progress over time, but for which there is a risk of overlapping lines (and thus illegibility) when too many entities are graphed or too-similar entities are graphed.

Other graph dilemmas, such as bar graphs that run off the page, also require considering how many entities are graphed. When graphing more than eight subgroups, consider rotating the graph or breaking one graph into two (Bernhardt, 2004). Other options include finding a more effective graph type or table for higher numbers of entities or else limiting the number of entities that can be displayed on the graph.

Consider how the above graphing guidelines can be applied to aid accurate understanding of the data it graphs:

See **Examples** E and F again. Example E (Before) does graph the data, but it commits many graphing infractions while doing so. Example E (Before) *looks* easy to read, but it is not the best graph for the job. It does not graph the appropriate data—i.e., the difference between Site and SMP, which is what truly communicates performance on this particular test and thus gives the data meaning. Thus Example E (Before) does not best facilitate key comparisons or appropriate analysis.

Example E (Before) also fails to use a scale beginning with 0, which distorts the data and makes comparisons to other graphs more difficult. While Example E (Before) does not use 3-D rotation, it does use 3-D shadows, which contribute to clutter within the graph and can distort size perception. It also fails to place percentages directly on the graph. Example F (After) solves all of these problems and also does a better job graphing entities, opting to use five bars in place of twenty yet still communicating more information.

Standard 4.2.05: Clear Headers

Use headers (e.g., cells that top report columns and start rows) that: (a) provide added info to prevent user confusion or the need to look elsewhere to understand the data's nature; (b) distinguish/group data (e.g., when there are varied categories of data columns, such as three columns of data for one test and three columns of data for another, use multiple header

Package/Display Standards: Report Design

rows to clarify demarcations and reduce text repetition); (c) avoid all caps (only use all capital letters if absolutely necessary to help distinguish some headers from others); and (d) repeat when printed (column headings should repeat at the top of each subsequent page when a table continues on multiple printed pages, just as main page header info should repeat and be included with page numbers).

Headers (the cells that top report columns and start rows) are like road signs when you are driving: they tell you what to expect where, and help you know where to go to see specific things. Without clear road signs, we would spend a lot of wasted time driving up and down streets before reaching our desired destination. Likewise, missing or unclear headers on data reports waste educators' time.

Provide Added Info

Headers can shrewdly provide information that prevents educators from having to look elsewhere for information, answers questions they might have, and avoids possible confusion or misunderstandings.

When filters do not narrow the origin of listed entities (e.g., the report was not run only for the "Science 1B" course, and thus it was run for multiple courses), row headers are a great place for giving additional details in a smaller, lighter, less prominent manner. For example, if each teacher has a row of results for each course he or she taught and these courses vary, the course name can be displayed under the teacher's name, but they should look as if they share the same row, with the teacher's name prominently in the row header (the first cell of the row), and the teacher's course's name under his or her name in smaller gray font. The example below illustrates this.

See **Examples** C and D again. The Example D (After) column header gives some added details in a smaller/non-bold font to let users know which information this column summarizes. With a small number of characters, the Example D (After) header answers the question many educators have concerning what criteria determine proficiency on a particular test, but does so unobtrusively so the many educators who already know this information can easily ignore it.

118

> On the bottom row, it is more helpful for educators to know the total (as opposed to average) number of students district-wide scoring within each level, so this is what the Example D (After) table features. Since this deviates from the row's key behavior of averaging the percent of students within each level, this deviation is indicated in a smaller/non-bold font underneath the row header's main verbiage.
>
> With a small number of characters, this Example D (After) header will help educators avoid confusion. Likewise, the many educators who can already guess how the row is presenting data can easily ignore the added detail, since it is featured as unobtrusively as it is in the other rows.

Distinguish/Group Data

The role of headers becomes more complex when there are varied categories of data columns. For example, when a report displays three columns of data belonging to one test and three columns of data belonging to another, the data are at risk of getting confused. In these cases, multiple header rows can be extremely helpful.

> See **Examples** A and B again. Check out the Example A (Before) column headers. Yikes! Single cells are crammed too full of information, making them hard to read, and it is very difficult to determine where the groups of data (e.g., three columns for each group/domain) exist. Example B (After) uses multiple rows/levels to break header information into manageable chunks while simultaneously establishing where each group's/domain's columns start and end.

Avoid All Caps

Unless all letters of a term are ordinarily capitalized (such as an acronym like AYP), avoid all capital letters in a header unless absolutely necessary to distinguish some headers from others. A study of reporting practices in 30 U.S. states resulted in the recommendation to use headings for different

119

report sections but to avoid "all caps," which make specific text harder to find (Aschbacher & Herman, 1991).

Repeat When Printed

A report that appears whole on one computer screen can be split into multiple pages when the report is printed. It is thus important for headers to behave in a helpful manner on the printed version:

- Page header information concerning input control selections (e.g., Which test year did the educator select when generating the report? Were all students included in the report or did the educator opt to include only Asian students? etc.) should print near the top of the report's first page or all pages. Page number (e.g., "Page 2 of 4") should appear on every page.
- Column headings should almost always repeat at the top of each subsequent page when a table continues on multiple pages.

Design

Standard 4.3.01: Format/Components Most Appropriate for Analysis

Select the format and components most likely to encourage accurate understanding/analysis/use of the data. For example, you might opt to use a table to communicate large amounts of data a report requires, but particular columns within the table can contain horizontal graph bars to highlight important data.

A large portion of educators are already intimidated by data. Many teachers and administrators do not know fundamental analysis concepts, and 70 percent have never taken a college or postgraduate course in educational measurement (Zwick et al., 2008). Only three states have implemented policies and practices ensuring educators know how to analyze and use data appropriately (National Association of States Boards of Education, 2012). For example, few teacher preparation programs cover topics such as state data literacy (Halpin & Cauthen, 2011; Stiggins, 2002).

Package/Display Standards: Report Design

In fact, few educators are trained statisticians who automatically know how to use available data effectively (Data Quality Campaign, 2009), and most people responsible for analyzing data have received no training to do so (Few, 2008). This is even the case among administrators, even though principals rate the ability to use data as the most important skill needed to be a good principal (Metropolitan Life Insurance Company, 2013).

Fortunately, these challenges can be reduced by good design. Consider the role design can play in making data analysis easier and less intimidating:

- Teachers are far more likely to use data if it is presented in a user-friendly format (Rennie Center for Education Research and Policy, 2006).

- Reporting format impacts how useful data is to stakeholders (Hamilton & Koretz, 2002).

- Improving a data system's design and reporting can ease some of the growing pains that occur as teachers increase their use of a data system (Underwood et al., 2008).

There is a distinction between designing reports and designing reports in a way that assists analyses.

Design recommendations for making data reports that work for educators could fill multiple books. Thus the OTCD Standards contained in this book focus on design decisions that are commonly poorly navigated by DSRPs and/or when existing design research that is not exclusive to education is difficult to apply to education-specific data reports. OTCD *Design* Standards focus on avoiding common design mishaps to which data systems and reports often fall victim, to the detriment of educators' data analyses.

Sometimes it is not just a matter of including graphics, but including the *right* graphics. Sometimes you know the right tables and graphs to include in a report, yet the way in which you include them (e.g., order and layout) can help or hurt educators' ability to use the data effectively. Format is one of the most important aspects of report design when making data reports that work for educators. Thus format and components comprise an important aspect of OTCD Standards.

Consider the following example to see how just one report element can have a great impact on educators' ability to use the displayed data effectively:

121

Package/Display Standards: Report Design

See **Examples** E and F again. Adhering to Standard 4.3.01 is the most important change between Example E (Before) and Example F (After).

To garner value from the data for this particular assessment in Example E (Before), educators had to subtract each score for SMP or (though less reliable due to smaller sample size) the SMA from each score for the site. Since the sum of those calculations is what suggests possible strengths/weaknesses, Example F (After) graphs those totals—the most important data—for the user. Note all other values from Example E (Before) are still featured in Example F (After), along with the new (and more important) values as points of comparison, but they are graphed less obtrusively since they are less important.

Even though Example F (After) might look harder to understand than Example E (Before), it is actually easier for the educator to make correct analyses (it is not worth looking easier if a graph leads to wrong analyses!). Even if the user does not spend more than five seconds trying to understand Example F (After), he or she can instantly guess which of Site's scores are worse (red, lower/negative numbers) and which are better (green, higher/positive numbers). Remember these examples are shown in color online.

Note how well the footer and an effective format work together. The footer that was added to Example F (After) is 220 characters (with spaces), which is well within the footer length limitation of 328 characters (including spaces) for landscape/horizontally orientated reports discussed in the "Label Standards" chapter of this book. Without the footer, users might be confused by this report's format, and without the improved format, some users would disregard the footer's caution to analyze the data in a way that is more complicated (but necessary for accurate analysis) than the easier-yet-wrong way the Example E (Before) report format encourages. Together, the footer and improved format work best to ensure accurate analysis of the data.

Standard 4.3.02: Avoid Clutter

Avoid unnecessary clutter, following guidelines such as: (a) do not outline bars/wedges if perimeters can survive bad printers (e.g., don't add a black line around a graph's red bar if the red is dark enough to be seen when printed on an old black and white printer); (b) use lines sparingly and purposefully (e.g., to distinguish sections of data rather than outlining every cell in a table); (c) include white space to make the report easy to understand (but not so much that it adds to excessive report pages when printed); (d) round numbers that will not lose distinctions (i.e., round all numbers to the whole unless you are dealing with small numbers for which distinctions will be lost without decimals, such as averages of performance levels ranging from just 1–5; when an extra place value is warranted, limit the decimals to one if effective); (e) show data and eliminate other clutter (i.e., if added data will give a report more meaning, add the data and select other clutter to eliminate); (f) avoid unnecessary text/columns/rows (e.g., if adding a table column with the calculation of performance-level data comprising percent Proficient, there is typically no need to add a column for the calculation of performance-level data comprising percent Not Proficient); and (g) not everything experts ask for has to be included (there are too many "recommended" additions for reports to accommo-date; consider each addition against the importance of avoiding report clutter).

Clutter can make data harder to read, important findings easier to miss, and the process of data analysis longer and more frustrating. Clutter can be caused by any contents (lines, text, color, images, etc.) that are unnecessary, used in overabundance, and/or placed poorly. Examples follow that illustrate how reports are improved when clutter is removed.

> - See **Examples** A and B again. Example A (Before) has many clutter infractions. By repeating the same information in each column's header (rather than using multiple heading levels), the column headers are too cluttered to read. By placing lines around every border on every cell, the table is covered in lines rather than letting fewer lines distinguish different areas of the table. Also, the added decimals are not needed anywhere but in the summaries (and they

would not be needed there either if the numbers were not so numerically small) and merely make the table too cluttered to easily compare data. See how Example B (After) solves each of these problems.

- See **Examples** C and D again. Example C (Before) had an unnecessarily long header. Example D (After) shortens this by using "%" instead of Percent and "#" instead of Number, since these symbols are so easily understood. "&" would have been used rather than "and", as well, except for the fact that "% & #" would look confusing. Since the test name is so widely known by the report's audience, its abbreviation can be used in the header as long as its full name is written out elsewhere (e.g., the report's abstract, interpretation guide, etc.). Also, minor cell borders were removed from Example D (After), which reduced clutter.

- See **Examples** E and F again. Example F (After) reduces clutter by graphing five bars instead of twenty (using lines, instead, for the less important values) and also by removing the legend and communicating its information, instead, through the title and the labels next to the graphed lines. 3-D/shadows were also removed.

The need to avoid clutter seems straightforward, but there are some aspects of clutter removal that are debated, with evidence on both sides of each argument. When applied to data systems used, specifically, in education, it is possible to break each tie and lean toward a single recommendation. However, it is helpful to know both sides for those rare cases where a different design decision is warranted:

Do Not Outline Bars/Wedges If Perimeters Survive Bad Printers

This one has valid arguments on both sides, so a compromise must be struck. Consider the pros and cons of adding a darker (e.g., black, gray, or a darker version of the color being used) line around the outside of a graph's bars or wedges, as well as the verdict:

Package/Display Standards: Report Design

Table 6.1

Argument Against	Argument For	Recommendation
Added lines add clutter. Let the color comprising each bar's "fill" speak for itself.	Many reports are printed and viewed outside of the data system rather than online (e.g., when a department coach prints teachers' reports for them—a common practice whether it is good practice or not). Many educators are using outdated printers, and budget restrictions cause ink cartridge and toner supplies to dwindle and sometimes stop. Thus print quality varies widely and colors of varying darkness can be hard to see when print quality is bad. In addition, some people are color-blind and cannot distinguish between red and green, causing problems if green and red graph portions are displayed directly next to one another (Bernhardt, 2004).	Both sides are valid. Avoid outlines if the graphic shapes will survive (with visible perimeters) a bad print job. Otherwise, consider a dark or gray outline around each bar or wedge on a graph. Its added clutter is minimal. Also, only 2% of educators are likely to be color-blind, and EnChroma glasses can allow most color-blind to see and distinguish colors (see details later in this chapter).

Use Lines Sparingly and Purposefully

The concept of using lines sparingly is a widely accepted means of avoiding clutter. However, it is sometimes disputed when it comes to outlining each cell in a table. Consider the pros, cons, and verdict:

Table 6.2

Argument Against	Argument For	Recommendation
Added lines add clutter. Do not use them to separate cells in a table.	Without lines, it can be hard for users to follow which data line up with which headings. Also, since research supports "data density," different types of information can run together.	Use lines sparingly and purposefully to distinguish sections of data (like *After* examples in this chapter).

125

Package/Display Standards: Report Design

Using lines purposefully (such as to distinguish sections of data) also requires consideration of placement. Some reports use an appropriate number of lines, but they are placed haphazardly (not lining up when they could have lined up, creating white space between report segments that is not evenly sized when it could have been evenly sized, etc.). This causes chaos-based clutter. To avoid these problems, adhere to a grid and follow basic design principles when formatting a report and its lines.

White Space without Excessive Pages

Consider the pros, cons, and verdict of added "white space," meaning areas on reports and documents where no "ink" (images, text, etc.) is featured so the eye can rest:

Table 6.3

Argument Against	Argument For	Recommendation
56% of educators are reading printed versions of reports that others used the data system to generate (Underwood et al., 2008). School budgets are limited; more white space means more paper waste.	Some of the main problems with data reports are information overload, report density, and clutter; rather, reports should use white space and variation to make reports appear easy to understand (NRC, 2001).	This one requires balance. Try to work in adequate white space while simultaneously trying to limit the number of report pages.

126

Round Numbers that Will Not Lose Distinctions

Often numbers in education data do not round evenly to whole numbers. Consider the pros, cons, and verdict of displaying numbers with decimals and additional place values:

Table 6.4

Argument Against	Argument For	Recommendation
Round numbers in almost all cases for ease of use (Goodman & Hambleton, 2004; Wainer, 1992, 1997). Decimals cause clutter and make numbers harder to compare.	Decimals are more specific. For example, if a table shows how sites performed in terms of student proficiency levels and the levels run from 1 to 4, rounding such small numbers will prevent users from seeing important discrepancies between site performance.	Round numbers as much as you can without losing meaning (Tufte, 2011). More specifically, round all numbers to the whole number *unless* you are dealing with small numbers for which distinctions will be lost without decimals. For example, if classes contain averages of performance levels ranging from just 1 to 5, and thus the averages show almost every class at a 3 in whole number format, an extra place value is warranted. In those cases, limit the decimal places to one if possible. If you display scores ranging from 1 to 50, however, skip the decimals altogether.

Package/Display Standards: Report Design

Choose Showing Numbers/Data over Other Clutter

With Tufte's (2011) call for "data density" echoed by other experts, the call for reduced clutter can seem in disagreement. Consider the pros, cons, and verdict for adding data to reports (e.g., displaying numbers, percentages, etc.):

Table 6.5

Argument Against	Argument For	Recommendation
Displaying more data on reports (e.g., numbers on graphs and tables) clutters the reports.	While the many pitfalls of clutter should be avoided, reports should maximize data density by presenting many numbers in a small space (Tufte, 2011).	Display more data when it will give the report more meaning and/or function. Eliminate other clutter to make room.

There is generally little or no debate concerning the remaining recommendations in this section:

Avoid Unnecessary Text/Columns/Rows

Many clutter-based decisions relate not to graphical elements, but to text. For example, there is rarely need to calculate all struggling performance levels to render a % Not Proficient column on a table when you are already calculating all proficiency levels to render a % Proficient column. To do so would be repetitive. Also, expanding the height of rows or the width of columns is preferable to adding empty rows or columns.

Not Everything Experts Ask For

Other clutter problems relate to attempts to accommodate all recommendations. Remember the extensive evidence for adding textual support to data reporting environments. There are far too many "recommended" additions to add to reports. If all of those recommendations were followed, the reports would be far too cluttered to communicate data effectively.

128

Such recommendations also include national standards, which have been available over the past two decades to offer guidance concerning the best ways to communicate test results:

- National Council on Measurement in Education, Code of Professional Responsibilities in Educational Measurement: Responsibilities of Those Who Interpret, Use, and Communicate Assessment Results (National Council on Measurement in Education, 1995): http://ncme.org/resource-center/code-of-professional-responsibilities-in-educational-measurement/
- American Educational Research Association (AERA) Standards for Educational and Psychological Testing (American Educational Research Association, American Psychological Association, & National Council on Measurement in Education, 1999): www.apa.org/science/programs/testing/standards.aspx (accessed October 30, 2015).
- Code of Fair Testing Practices in Education Reporting and Interpreting Test Results (Joint Committee on Testing Practices, 2004): www.apa.org/science/programs/testing/fair-code.aspx

Just like literature profiled in this book's "Label Standards" chapter, national standards applicable to data systems and reports indicate an overwhelming amount of information that should accompany test results. However, note this information does not necessarily have to be crammed onto the report itself. Rather, remember how supplemental documentation and the help system can help house added information.

Like other research-based recommendations, national standards' requirements should be balanced against the importance of avoiding report clutter. Since research notes how easily educators can be overwhelmed by including too much information in reports,[1] reports need to include only those features most effective in improving each unique dataset's analysis.

Conclusion

By cutting unnecessary clutter from reports, you leave room for the data to be more clear. You also enable any added information (clutter that is "worth it" to ensure proper analysis) to have the room it needs to be effective.

Package/Display Standards: Report Design

Standard 4.3.03: Avoid Keys/Legends

Work content into a chart's title or labels (e.g., directly within or beside graph segments such as bars or lines) to avoid a key or legend whenever possible. If legend inclusion is unavoidable, keep the order of colors/explanations in the key consistent with the order in which segments are presented in the graph.

Every time a chart requires a user to look away, find a key or legend, gather knowledge on a color or character's meaning, and then look back at the chart again to apply that knowledge . . . it risks losing the user. In addition, legends do not work well when their colors have to be printed in black and white. Whenever content can be worked into the chart's title or labels, or directly within or beside the graph segments (e.g., bars or wedges), a key or legend should be avoided.

> See **Examples** E and F again. The key from Example E (Before) is easily overlooked by users, will not work well if the graph is printed in black and white, adds clutter, and requires users to look away from the data and back again to make sense of it. If the graph format had been good, all of the key's data could instead be placed inside the graph's bars. Example F (After) eliminates the key and instead communicates its information through the title and the labels next to the graphed lines.

There are a few cases where a legend is needed. For example, keys can be needed when a report contains a line graph with lines that overlap (creating little room for within-graph labels), particularly if they overlap at the start and end of the lines, where labels are typically most effective on line graphs. If a report containing a line graph is dynamic, meaning users have the option of generating the report in a number of ways (such as for different sets of students), it is nearly impossible to place labels in a way that will work well for any scenario. Thus a key/legend could be warranted in these cases. If including a legend is unavoidable, at least keep the order of colors/explanations in the key consistent with the order in which bars, lines, or wedges are presented in the graph.

130

Package/Display Standards: Report Design

Standard 4.3.04: Most Important Data in Prime Locations

Place the report's most important data in places likely to stand out (e.g., not lost in a table's middle columns). Treat the last column or row in a table as prime real estate, reserved for data users are most likely to need. Treat the first row and column (which come after the header row and column) as slightly less prime (but more desirable than middle columns) if additional data needs to stand out. Likewise, reserve any culminating graphics or sections for those communicating key info.

Reports contain areas that can be considered "prime real estate," as the user's eyes fall more immediately and/or frequently on these locations. Thus the user can more easily survey information from these locations. For example:

- Content at the **top of the report** is seen more easily and readily than content at the end of the report. This is especially true when the report involves scrolling within a data system or page turning when in printed format.

- Content at the **end of the report** often stands out more than content sandwiched in the middle. Since some summarizing visuals are more appropriate after other details have been viewed, this provides a good place for graphs that summarize key data.

- The **last column or row** in a table is prime real estate, as it is easy to see and less cluttered than those sandwiched in the middle.

- The **first row and column** are also prime real estate, but these are typically being used already for column and row headers. The first data column following row headers in a table can thus serve as real estate less prime than the last columns but more prime than the middle columns.

Reports should not culminate with data less important than that in other areas (a common culprit is "# tested," which often steals prime locations in education data reports but is rarely the most important data). Vital data (often the averages or sums to which other data can be compared) should stand out. Likewise, any culminating graphics or information should summarize important concepts, not trifles.

131

Designing where particular datasets will go on a report takes logic and an awareness of what educators want to achieve when using a particular report. For example:

- Which stakeholders will use the report?
- What will users want to do with the report?
- What will users want to know from the report?
- What actions will users want the report to inform?

Whoever designs the report must know the most prevalent answers to these questions as pertains to the specific report being designed.

Reports must communicate data in a logical order (Wainer, 1992) and assign report space based on the importance of what is being displayed (Aschbacher & Herman, 1991). Following these design guidelines results in reports allowing educators to more easily find information and group or differentiate information. This saves users time and allows the report to be more effective.

Bending Limitations

Sometimes a data system utilizes software (e.g., reporting software) that places some limitations on where different report aspects can and cannot be placed. In cases like these, adhering to other Package/Display standards can compensate for this data having to be forced into prime locations.

For example, the particular software in use might require that "# tested" (*rarely* the most important data being communicated) be displayed first, such as in the first non-header row or column of a table. In that case someone might feel forced to live with a display like that shown in Example G (Before) (in color online).

Unfortunately, the Example G display makes *# tested* (in the second column and second row) appear at least—if not more—important than the other data displayed. Check out the revised version of the table in Example H (After) (also in color online). The improved table does not involve moving or removing any of the data from the poorly displayed table in Example G (Before). Instead, Example H (After) utilized the following tricks to make *# tested* data less obtrusive:

- A **cell border (i.e., a line)** is not added between the *# tested* row and the row above it, nor is a cell border/line added between the *# tested* column and the column before it. Rather, lines are used to fool the eye into treating data in the *# tested* cells as just other parts of the header cells.
- **Color and shading** are used to absorb *# tested* data into the header cells and make the eye see only the percent cells as the data focus. This can be seen better where the examples are in color (online).
- The **size** of *# tested* data is reduced to indicate it is less important than the other data presented.

The *# tested* data is a useful reference and remains available, but now the eye can scan across *key* data during analysis without less important data adding clutter and getting in the way. The display is still simple but much more effective, and the display format is more appropriate for the analysis of this particular data.

% of Students Scoring at Each Performance Level	# Tested	All Students	Socioec. Disadv.	English Learner	Students with Disab.
# Tested	392	392	101	32	13
Proficient & Advanced	169	43%	21%	22%	8%
Advanced	52	13%	9%	6%	0%
Proficient	117	30%	12%	16%	8%
Basic	92	23%	31%	38%	23%
Below Basic	59	15%	18%	22%	23%
Far Below Basic	72	18%	31%	19%	46%

Figure 6.7 Example G (Before)

Package/Display Standards: Report Design

% of Students Scoring at Each Performance Level with # Tested		All Students 392	Socioec. Disadv. 101	English Learner 32	Students with Disab. 13
Proficient & Advanced	169	43%	21%	22%	8%
Advanced	52	13%	9%	6%	0%
Proficient	117	30%	12%	16%	8%
Basic	92	23%	31%	38%	23%
Below Basic	59	15%	18%	22%	23%
Far Below Basic	72	18%	31%	19%	46%

Figure 6.8 Example H (After)

Standard 4.3.05: Juxtapose Comparisons

Offer reports that juxtapose multiple subgroups, other entities, years/ times, or measures for easy comparison (i.e., users should not have to run separate reports to make common comparisons). Use proximity within reports when placing data that will need to be compared.

If teacher Anita Book disaggregates a report by English Learner (EL) and finds her ELs averaged 79 percent correct on a test, will Anita think this percent (considered with other measures and factors, of course) is reason for celebration or concern? Chances are Anita will want to look at growth (e.g., a report that shows the same students' performance over time) or to compare the EL students to non-EL students.

The answer to the last question is thus another question:

> How did Anita's EL students perform in relation to fluent students or in relation to previous performance?

If Anita is using a report that pertains only to EL students rather than juxtaposing EL results next to fluent students' results, or pertains only to a single point in time, Anita will not know the answers to her questions. The 79 percent is meaningless without other subgroups' performance or performance from other years. This is because context gives data meaning, and comparison provides important context.

While a data system should allow educators to disaggregate its reports (e.g., run a report just for students with certain attributes), it should also offer reports comparing multiple subgroups with their results juxtaposed next to one another for added meaning. The same goes for reports that juxtapose multiple entities (e.g., students, teachers, etc.), multiple years or other benchmark periods, and multiple measures.

Research shows that when educators have to draw comparisons between data featured in different reports, the quality of their analyses declines. For example, through case study, Knights et al. (2014) found fragmented data with multiple-page formats that prevent comparison also prevented education data displays from facilitating decision-making. Educators should not have to run separate reports to make comparisons; rather, running a report for a single subgroup or measure should be something educators do when they want to delve deeper into a particular entity or measurement.

Standard 4.3.06: Eye Can Scan Without Obstacles

Allow the user's eye to move across a report or section without encountering visual obstacles that impede common comparisons. For example, if accompanying a table's primary data (such as rows for "% of students" earning each column's performance level) with secondary data (such as rows for "# of students" earning each column's performance level), give secondary data a smaller font so it is easy to ignore or compare separately when the eye scans the page.

More than one number is on a report because you are meant to view and compare numerous data. Design should not get in the way of this, and it does not matter whether you are designing a graph, a table, a figure, or something else. Clutter is often the culprit, but often the solution lies in removing clutter while also finding a better report format. Consider these examples, particularly the first:

- See **Examples** C and D again. Look at the cluttered mess of characters within each cell of the Example C (Before) table, with contents such as "29% (73)". Try to compare percentages of students from one performance level to the next. See how the parenthetical numbers get in the way, even though they are the least important data in this report and only there for ancillary information? Now view the Example D (After) table. See how freely your eye can now scan from one percentage to the next? The numbers are still there, but they no longer vie for the primary attention they do not warrant.

- See **Examples** E and F again. All of the graph bars in Example E (Before) look equally important, and the clutter of 20 bars makes it hard to compare a single entity's performance from one cluster/category to the next. In contrast, Example F (After) gives bars only to the most important data, so users can easily compare the site's performance in each cluster. Likewise, in Example F (After), the use of lines above 0 for SMA data, lines below 0 for State Average data, and SMP data as the 0 point allows easier viewing of that data, too. This arrangement was crafted in accordance with analysis guidelines from this particular assessment's author.

The design of reports should show sensitivity to how educators need to view each particular set of data. When educators look at a report, it should be easy to compare what they want to compare, and easy to focus on the data that matters most. If not, the reports likely need to do a better job of allowing the user's eye to scan the data it needs without obstacles.

How "Dynamic Sorting" Works

When a report is displayed within a data system and the user clicks a column header, the table re-sorts its rows into numerical order (e.g., low-to-high) based on the values in that column. If the user clicks the same column header again, the order reverses (e.g., high-to-low).

Package/Display Standards: Report Design

Extra Consideration

Do not overlook how the first example on page 136 impacts dynamic sorting if the report is displayed within a data system. The DSRP should base sort order on the larger, more important value. The two values originally stacked together should remain stacked together. In other words, dynamic sorting should not group all the percentages together and all the numbers together.

Standard 4.3.07: Do Not Hug Lines

With few exceptions (such as widely varying figures), center or indent data horizontally within cells and center data vertically within cells rather than justifying data directly against cell borders.

Numbers and percentages should almost always be centered in cells or indented rather than left- or right-justified directly against the cell borders, and all text should be vertically centered within cells. The added space makes them easier to read and removes clutter, making comparisons easier. Note this does not usually mean contents should be centered across *multiple* cells (e.g., if cell A1 will serve as the row header for rows 1–4, keep it vertically centered in row 1 and *not* centered across merged rows 1–4).

See **Examples** C and D again. Example C (Before) left-justifies data within the cells, making the data harder to read and compare, and less inviting to users. By centering the data, Example D (After) creates white space padding within the cells without adding to the size of the table.

Centering works well when all numbers are close in size (e.g., all two digits, all three digits, all one-to-two digits, etc.). If data size varies widely (or, as with some dynamic reports, has the potential to vary widely) within a single generated report and/or you have to left-justify for a reason, indent the data slightly so it does not sit directly against the cell wall.

Standard 4.3.08: Purposeful Color and Shading

Use color and shading purposefully and selectively (a) as an additional layer of communication (e.g., bars of graphed scores can be green vs. red to visually communicate if the scores rendered *Proficient* vs. *Not Proficient* status) and (b) to help organize a report (e.g., report section headings can be shaded to stand out and better differentiate sections).

Humans are visual creatures who rely on their visual systems to distinguish relationships, differences, and more (Kosslyn, 2006). Color is an additional layer of communication that manages its task with minimal (if any) added clutter. This is not something other means of communication can easily claim. For example, a traffic light can tell you to stop or go without adding any elements, such as extra words or images; rather, it merely changes the color of the existing element—the light—in order to send a clear message.

Likewise, a graph could present bars of score data in the same shade, but if the bars were colored based on the success of the score (e.g., if it indicated the student was struggling vs. proficient vs. advanced in an area), the user would receive instant, additional information without the clutter of added text or images.

Color and/or shading can also be used to organize a report, such as by making headings stand out, differentiating between different report sections, helping users follow a row of data across multiple columns, or differentiating between different types of information being presented (e.g., a "how to" heading on a green heading bar vs. a "warning" heading on a red heading bar).

Just like other report elements, however, color and shading should be used selectively and with purpose. If you slather a report with every color of the rainbow, each color's ability to stand out (and thus the ability of the meaning you are attaching to the color to stand out) is reduced if not negated.

To use color and shading purposefully in reports, consider:

- what added information you wish to communicate (or wish to make stand out) with color or shading;

- if color/shading is the best means of communicating this information, or if color/shading would be better served communicating other information in the report;

Package/Display Standards: Report Design

- which colors/shades would best communicate this information (e.g., green means desirable performance—as in ready to "go" forward—whereas the closer a color moves from yellow to orange to red it means less desirable performance—as in "stop" and do something about it);
- how users will know the colors' or shades' meaning;
- how this meaning can remain consistent across reports.

It also helps for colors and shades to have contrast (e.g., for cases where reports have to be printed in black and white, or due to some users' color blindness), but this need becomes less dire when keys/legends are eliminated and graph elements (such as bars, lines, or wedges) are labeled directly (as recommended in the "Avoid Keys/Legends" section of this chapter). This is especially true in cases where graph elements do not overlap (e.g., bars or pie wedges), as long as the elements feature outlines (as recommended in the "Avoid Clutter" section). However, contrast should still be high in cases where there is overlap (e.g., intersecting lines on a line graph, or abutting points on a scatterplot) or a key/legend is unavoidable.

Consider some examples of how color and shading can improve reports (remember color versions of these examples are online):

- See **Examples** A and B again. Example A (Before) made some attempts at color use, but so many more opportunities were missed. Example B (After) uses color to make numbers and proficiency status's meanings stand out (red = undesirable, green = desirable), making it easier to spot differences and similarities. "After" also uses shading to distinguish between heading levels, make summary rows stand out, and help users keep track of each student's row now that the clutter of too many lines has been removed.

- See **Examples** C and D again. Both Example C (Before) and Example D (After) appropriately colored the red-to-green headers to correlate with performance levels moving from undesired (red) to desired (green) and beyond (dark green). Example D (After) uses shading (rather than lines) on rows and to make column and row summary information stand out as different (e.g., comparison points).

Package/Display Standards: Report Design

> ● See **Examples** E and F again. Because of the way data is graphed in Example E (Before), color has to be used to distinguish one entity from the next (e.g., Site vs. State Average). Conversely, graphing just one entity (but without losing any data) frees up Example F (After) to use color in a more powerful way. Example F (After) can then communicate meaning with each graph bar's color: red when Site's scores are worse (lower/negative numbers), and green when they are better (higher/positive numbers). This way, even if the user does not thoroughly understand the graph, he or she can instantly guess how Site performed in each cluster/category. Also, since other data (from the state) is present in Example F (After) but less important, simple gray lines are used to graph it (rather than colored bars).

Conflicting Arguments

A common argument against relying on color use is color blindness, which could affect some users. This is not as alarming a problem within education and data reporting as some make it seem because:

● Color blindness, which in its most common form diminishes the ability to distinguish green from red, affects 7 percent of men in the U.S. but only 0.4 percent of women (Montgomery, 2013). Since 75 percent of educators are female (Papay, Harvard Graduate School of Education, 2007), this means only 2 percent of educators are likely to be color-blind. In addition, EnChroma glasses compensate for all but the rarest cases of color blindness, allowing the color-blind to distinguish the colors they previously could not, and are thus becoming increasingly popular among the color-blind.

● Even without EnChroma glasses, color blindness would only be a problem in reporting if a report's meaning *relied* on color recognition. As noted above, using color offers an *added* layer of meaning, such as extra help knowing when a new section has started, or extra help noting which scores are good and which are less desirable. However, if this book's design standards are fully followed (such as by avoiding keys—and thus avoiding the need to associate particular colors with particular

Package/Display Standards: Report Design

graph constructs—in favor of labeling graph constructs directly, displaying data values directly on graphs, adding footers to explain how to read the report, etc.), the report's meaning and implications can be figured out without color. If you absolutely must rely on color as the sole source of meaning (e.g., if a key/legend is for some reason unavoidable), visit http://colorlab.wickline.org/ to select a color palette that can be distinguished by the color blind.

Color use is highly recommended. Implement this book's other *Design* standards, as well, so the color adds an added layer (rather than a required layer) of understanding. This way the 2 percent of educators who are color-blind *and* who do not have EnChroma glasses can still benefit from the reports. The same goes for the greater percent of other stakeholders—e.g., students or parents—who might be viewing data displays designed for non-educator audiences.

Standard 4.3.09: Size Reflects Importance

If there are any required variations in size (e.g., font size), make sure it is appropriate for users to deem the reduced-size info as less important.

Imagine you are driving. As you are about to turn the corner, you notice two signs:

- One sign communicates parking is off-limits on Tuesdays from 1:00–2:00 a.m. due to street-sweeping.
- The other sign communicates "Do Not Enter; Wrong Way" because you almost turned onto the wrong end of a one-way street.

With that image in your mind, answer this question:

Which sign was larger and more prominent (the parking sign or the wrong-way sign)?

The wrong way sign should have been larger and more prominent than the parking sign, because it was more important. The consequences of you inconveniencing street sweepers with your parking job are not as dire (or possibly fatal) as the consequences of you barreling into oncoming, unsuspecting traffic.

Package/Display Standards: Report Design

When a data report uses a large font for some text and a smaller font for other, it is sending a message to the educator concerning the text's importance. Smaller text is more easily ignored because it is being communicated as less important than text in larger font. This is why footers should be the same font size as the report's body/data, or else they could be ignored. Conversely, something less dire to the data's analysis (such as a copyright) can be smaller. Consider some examples:

- See **Examples** C and D again. Example C (Before) featured percent and number data in the same font size, so they competed for attention even though the numbers were much less important (mainly present to alert users if numbers were too small to warrant much significance). Example D (After) appropriately makes the numbers smaller so they do not interfere with analysis of the more important percentages.

- See **Examples** C and D again. Example C (Before) used the same font size for everything. In Example D (After), users will quickly get the hang of how columns 1–2 under each domain belong to the first and second year, and the third belongs to growth. Thus this information is only needed for initial or occasional reference and is less important than the domain names and main heading above them. A smaller font is therefore used in Example D (After) so its text does not clutter the header area.

- See **Examples** E and F again. Since State data in Example F (After) is less important than Site data, it is featured in smaller font size. This way it can still be present without getting in the way of analyses/comparisons, adding to clutter, or serving as a distraction from the more important data. Likewise, the Site's number for each cluster/category, garnered from the required calculation of subtracting the SMP percent from the Site percent, is the most important; thus it is featured in a bold, larger font in Example F (After). The Site's actual percent score is also featured in smaller, white font because it is less important than the graphed number but is sometimes needed for reference (e.g., when there is a cap on how big the number/sum can be due to scores of 100 percent).

142

Package/Display Standards: Report Design

If you see unimportant data (e.g., "# tested") communicated as equally important as—or worse, *more* important than—the data educators are most concerned with on a report (e.g., performance or demographics), your reports might not be doing a good job of conveying importance via size. Sometimes fixing the problem will involve other standards' recommendations concerning prominence, such as:

- removing cell wall lines above a top "# tested" row so it is absorbed by the header (and thus present but more easily ignored) rather than competing with the more important data for attention;
- adhering to established footer font size guidelines.

Thus other OTCD Standards covered in this book should be considered accordingly.

Standard 4.3.10: Not Unnecessarily Complicated or Overly Simplified

Do not make a report more complicated than it needs to be *or* more simple than it has to be. For example, use (a) a simple yet effective display (e.g., do not simplify the data presentation to the point that it is misunderstood or less effective) and (b) use simple language and avoid jargon (e.g., use *# tested* rather than *n, average* rather than *mean, growth* or *improvement* rather than *gain score, most frequent score* rather than *mode*, etc.).

Teacher and principal job satisfaction is dropping. Only 39 percent of teachers report they are very satisfied (the lowest in twenty-five years), 75 percent of school principals believe their jobs have become too complex, and half of teachers and principals report being regularly under great stress (Metropolitan Life Insurance Company, 2013). Fifty-five percent of teachers report their morale is low or very low, and 69 percent of teachers report morale has declined (National Union of Teachers, 2013). To be considerate of educators and the students they use data to help, do not make a report more complicated that it needs to be.

Simple Yet Effective Display

As Albert Einstein said to Louis Zukofsky, "Everything should be as simple as it can be, *but not simpler*" (later covered in Einstein, 1934). Sometimes

Package/Display Standards: Report Design

data is complicated, but you want its format (e.g., using a more familiar format) to be as unintimidating and inviting as possible. The challenge is that you must also make the data as easy to understand and analyze as possible. Keep this adage in mind:

Never favor simplifying a report in such a way that it increases the data's risk of being misunderstood, analyzed incorrectly, or misused.

See **Examples** E and F again. Example E (Before) can *look* simpler and more inviting, but its display is misleading and is thus more likely to result in faulty analysis. Example F (After) is thus more ideal, and other OTCD Standards have been added to make it easier to work with.

For example, if you gave an educator five seconds to look at the Example E (Before) graph and tell you the site's strengths, as indicated on this measure, he or she would likely either give you the wrong answer or else give you no answer, since five seconds is not enough time to make all the calculations necessary to determine the right answer when the data is displayed this way. Conversely, if you gave an educator five seconds to look at the Example F (After) graph and answer the same question, even if he or she did not understand why the data was graphed this way, his or her instant guess on the site's strengths would likely be right.

Simple Terms

T-scores, z-scores, etc. can sound great to statisticians and math whizzes, but they are rarely understood by educators with as much ease and confidence as terms such as "% correct." Unless an assessment's analysis requires advanced statistical terms, avoid them (and if they are required, explain them clearly in a prominent position).

When it comes to terms you must communicate, lend the same sensitivity to your word choice. For example:

- Use *# tested* rather than *n*.
- Use *average* rather than *mean*.

144

Package/Display Standards: Report Design

- Use *growth* or *improvement* rather than *gain score*.
- Use *most frequent score* rather than *mode*.

And so on. If there is an entire Wikipedia entry devoted to explaining a term, you should most likely look for better wording options.

This falls under the same guideline as avoiding statistical or education jargon. See the "Audience-Appropriate" section of the "Content Standards" chapter for more considerations related to word choice.

Note

1. Due to the quantity of support for this statement, please see related research in eResources.

References

Alverson, C. Y. (2008). *Exploring differences in teachers', administrators', and parents' preferences for data display and whether type of graphic display influences accuracy when extracting information.* University of Oregon. ProQuest Dissertations and Theses. Retrieved from http://search.proquest.com/docview/304502112 (accessed October 30, 2015).

American Educational Research Association, American Psychological Association, & National Council on Measurement in Education (1999). *Standards for educational and psychological testing.* Washington, DC: American Educational Research Association.

Aschbacher, P. R., & Herman, J. L. (1991). *Guidelines for effective score reporting* (CSE Technical Report 326). Los Angeles, CA: UCLA Center for Research on Evaluation, Standards, and Student Testing.

Bernhardt, V. L. (2004). *Data analysis for continuous school improvement.* Larchmont, NY: Eye on Education.

Clark, R., & Lyons, C. (2004). *Graphics for learning: Proven guidelines for planning, designing, and evaluating visuals in training materials.* San Francisco, CA: John Wiley & Sons.

Data Quality Campaign (2009). *The next step: Using longitudinal data systems to improve student success.* Retrieved from www.dataqualitycampaign.org/find-resources/the-next-step/ (accessed October 30, 2015).

Data Quality Campaign (2010). *Creating reports using longitudinal data: How states can present information to support student learning and school system improvement.* Retrieved from www.dataqualitycampaign.org/wp-content/uploads/files/1065_DQC%20Reports%20Issue%20Brief%20Nov8.pdf (accessed October 30, 2015).

Einstein, A. (1934, April). On the method of theoretical physics. *Philosophy of Science,* 1(2), 163–169.

Few, S. (2008, November 14). *Telling compelling stories with numbers: Data visualization for enlightening communication.* Statewide Longitudinal Data Systems (SLDS) Grant Program Third Annual Fall Grantee Meeting. Presentation conducted from SLDS, Arlington, VA. Retrieved from http://nces.ed.gov/programs/slds/pdf/08_F_06.pdf (accessed October 30, 2015).

Goodman, D. P., & Hambleton, R. K. (2004). Student test score reports and interpretive guides: Review of current practices and suggestions for future research. *Applied Measurement in Education,* 17(2), 145–220.

Halpin, J., & Cauthen, L. (2011, July 31). The education dashboard. *Center for Digital Education's Converge Special Report,* 2(3), 2–36.

Hamilton, L. S., & Koretz, D. M. (2002). Tests and their use in test-based accountability systems. In L. S. Hamilton, B. M. Stecher, & S. P. Klein (Eds.), *Making sense of test-based accountability in education,* 13–49. Santa Monica, CA: Rand.

Hattie, J. (2010). Visibly learning from reports: The validity of score reports. *Online Educational Research Journal.* Retrieved from www.oerj.org/View?action=view Paper&paper=6 (accessed October 30, 2015).

Joint Committee on Testing Practices (2004). *Code of fair testing practices in education.* Washington, DC: American Psychological Association. Retrieved from www.apa.org/science/programs/testing/fair-code.aspx (accessed October 30, 2015).

Jones, G. E. (2007). *How to lie with charts* (2nd ed.). Santa Monica, CA: LaPuerta.

Kosslyn, S. M. (2006). *Graph design for the eye and mind.* New York, NY: Oxford University Press, Inc.

Knights, G., Allee, W., & Center, B. (2014). *Developing decision-driving data displays: A case study at Newport-Mesa Unified School District.* California Educational Research Association (CERA) Conference. Presentation conducted from Paradise Point Resort, San Diego, CA.

Metropolitan Life Insurance Company (2013). *MetLife survey of the American teacher: Challenges for school leadership.* New York, NY: Author and Peanuts Worldwide.

Montgomery, G. (2013). *Breaking the code of color. Seeing, hearing, and smelling the world: New findings help scientists make sense of our senses: A report from the Howard Hughes Medical Institute,* 15–21. Howard Hughes Medical Institute: Chase, MD. Retrieved from www.hhmi.org/senses/b130.html (accessed May 7, 2013

National Association of States Boards of Education (2012, December). *Born in another time: Ensuring educational technology meets the needs of students today—and tomorrow*. Arlington, VA: Author.

National Council on Measurement in Education (1995). *Code of professional responsibilities in educational measurement*. Washington, DC: Author.

National Research Council (2001). *NAEP reporting practices: Investigating district-level and market-basket reporting*. Committee on NAEP Reporting Practices, Board on Testing and Assessment, Center for Education. Washington, DC: National Academy Press.

National Union of Teachers (2013, January 2). Teacher survey shows government going in wrong direction. Retrieved from www.teachers.org.uk/node/17250 (accessed October 30, 2015).

Outing, S., & Ruel, L. (2006, January 30). The best of Eyetrack III: What we saw when we looked through their eyes. *Eyetrack III*, 1–9. The Poynter Institute. Retrieved from www.academia.edu/546755/The_best_of_eyetrack_III_What_we_saw_when_we_looked_through_their_eyes (accessed October 30, 2015).

Papay, J., Harvard Graduate School of Education (2007). *Aspen Institute datasheet: The teaching workforce*. Washington, DC: The Aspen Institute.

Rennie Center for Education Research and Policy (2006, February). *Data-driven teaching: Tools and trends*. Cambridge, MA: Rennie Center for Education Research and Policy.

Sabbah, F. M. (2011). *Designing more effective accountability report cards*. ProQuest Dissertations and Theses, AAT 3469488. Retrieved from http://search.proquest.com/docview/893068662 (accessed October 30, 2015).

Stiggins, R. (2002). Assessment for learning. *Education Week*, 21(26), 30, 32–33.

Tufte, E. (2011, December 8) *Presenting data and information*. Presentation conducted from the Westin San Francisco Market Street, San Francisco, CA.

Underwood, J. (2013). Data visualization best practices. Retrieved from www.slideshare.net/idigdata/data-visualization-best-practices-2013 (accessed October 30, 2015).

Underwood, J. S., Zapata-Rivera, D., & VanWinkle, W. (2008) Growing pains: Teachers using and learning to use IDMS. *ETS Research Memorandum RM-08-07*. Princeton, NJ: ETS.

Wainer, H. (1992). Understanding graphs and tables. *Educational Researcher*, 21(1), 14–23.

Wainer, H. (1997). *Visual revelations: Graphical tales of fate and deception from Napoleon Bonaparte to Ross Perot*. New York, NY: Copernicus.

Zwick, R., Sklar, J., Wakefield, G., Hamilton, C., Norman, A., & Folsom, D. (2008). Instructional tools in educational measurement and statistics (ITEMS) for school personnel: Evaluation of three web-based training modules. *Educational Measurement: Issues and Practice*, 27, 14–27.

Package/Display Standards
User Interface

User Interface Aspects

While the last chapter focused specifically on data reports, this chapter covers the user interface, which affects how users access those reports and move between them. This chapter covers two key aspects to user interface: navigation and, specifically, input controls.

Navigation

Standard 4.4.01: Easy and Fast

Facilitate easy (e.g., logical arrangement) and fast/efficient (e.g., few clicks) use and movement within the system, remembering users' tech-familiarity varies.

Over-the-counter (i.e., easy) navigation allows educators to use and move through a data system or other reporting environment with ease. This involves:

- how educators move through the system and find reports (involving good design and the use of filters);
- how educators move from one report to the next (involving reports being consolidated to support multiple inquiries and also involving design consistency).

Data systems should offer a centralized, intuitive, user-friendly interface (in regards to navigation, drill down, data selection, and more) for accessing all reports (SAS Institute, 2013). *Intuitive* means most users can figure out where to find things and how to accomplish tasks within the system, simply due to the system's good design and logical placement/workings. For example:

- Items (buttons/links/etc.) should be placed in logical locations, where the user would most likely expect to find them. This arrangement is not limited to items within the same page, but also to how items are arranged across multiple pages (e.g., how one menu or link extends to submenus or other links, etc.). Navigation tools are most likely to be seen and used when placed at the top of a webpage (Outing & Ruel, 2006). This means the buttons or links users click to access reports (to share, build, print, customize, etc.) in the data system are typically featured at the top of the webpage, often within a navigation bar, though sometimes they appear on the side. This bar of navigation options commonly remains ever-present, even when the user scrolls down the page (i.e., the navigation options remain "frozen" even when the rest of the page changes).

- Moving through the system should be fast. This means the system should aim for few clicks (meaning times users click something with the mouse's cursor). However, clicks should not be so severely limited that the result is an overly crowded interface that is slow to navigate. For example, it would technically reduce all tasks to as few clicks as possible to place a link for every task imaginable on the same/home page. However, this would result in a screen that is crowded with thousands of links, within which it would be difficult and time-intensive to locate the desired link (defeating the purpose of limiting clicks). Thus the interface must strike a balance between easy-to-navigate placement and the need to limit clicks.

- The arrangement should work for as many users as possible, so it should not be assumed that every user is tech-savvy. For example, the tech-savvy programmers and developers who typically build a data system are not the only ones who need to find the system intuitive.

Package/Display Standards: User Interface

Educators are busy people, and any time that a data system steals from them by being slow or difficult to use is time that is stolen from the students educators want to use their time helping. If educators are using a suite of reports stemming from a simpler interface (e.g., printed, or housed within a single electronic menu), this standard applies to the report's arrangement and/or table of contents. Whatever the format, good navigation design that renders a system easy and fast to use is imperative.

Standard 4.4.02: Efficient Filters for Finding Reports

Provide filters users can select to narrow the list of available reports relevant to their needs. Provide filters that: (a) cover major search needs varied users are likely to have; (b) do not cover minor search needs (reserve this for open-ended searching); (c) utilize proper capitalization (for appearance) but do not operate on a case-sensitive basis (e.g., a lowercase search can lead to uppercase-tagged reports); (d) allow for multiple tags per report (tags are report-tied terms by which filters operate) and the ability to use multiple filters; (e) are displayed in clear, logical categories when users are viewing and selecting filters; and (f) are region-specific (to match the user's tests, etc.).

Filters help data system users find reports relevant to their needs. They can be added to a report search, or selected to narrow down a list of reports so it only lists reports that meet particular criteria.

For example, if a superintendent wants to know how many students in the district scored *Proficient* in Science on a state test called *State Test*, she would use the *State Test* filter so only reports capable of displaying State Test data would be listed for her for the moment. If she wanted to know this data over four years, she might also use the *3+ Years of Data* filter.

In addition to being **present**, report search filters should be efficient:

150

Package/Display Standards: User Interface

Filters for Major Needs

A data system should have enough filters to cover all major search needs. Note many of these needs are specific to region (e.g., if you live in Michigan you might want to view MEAP scores and thus need a MEAP filter, if you live in California you might want to view old CST scores and thus need a CST filter and not a MEAP filter, etc.). Examples are provided on the next page.

No Minor-Need Filters

A data system should not include a filter for every minor search need, or else you risk the disadvantages of clutter. Plus, if your report list allows for searches—which it should—users can easily type in a term and find a report that way if the word is embedded in the report title.

Proper Capitalization but Not Case Sensitive

Filters should use proper capitalization (for proper appearance and to be easily identified), but the filters should not operate on a case-sensitive basis. For example, if the data system allows for custom tags and User A tags a report as el (lowercase), and then User B runs a search for EL (uppercase) reports, User A's report should still appear in User B's search even though the capitalization differs.

Multiple Tags per Report

Data systems should have the ability to associate multiple tags/filters with a report, and should offer users the ability to use multiple filters. For example, Report A might be tagged as Attendance, Students, and Cohort Comparison, whereas Report B might be tagged as Attendance, Departments, and Cohort Comparison. If I ran a search using the filters Attendance and Cohort Comparison, both of these two reports would appear on my narrowed report list.

Package/Display Standards: User Interface

Categorized Filter Display

Filters should be displayed in clear, logical categories. For example, these filters are helpful, but jumbled together they are harder to use and some are too wordy (note some acronyms in this example are region-specific):

Filters	
1 Year's Data	Enrollment (Class Roster)
2 Years' Data	Grade Level Summary
3 or More Years' Data	Grade Levels Listed
API	Grades/GPA
Attendance	Health
AYP	Program/Group Summary
CAHSEE	Programs/Groups Listed
CELDT	School/Site Summary
Cohort Comparison	Schools/Sites Listed
Course Summary	STAR (CAPA/CMA/CST/STS)
Courses Listed	Student Summary
Class Period Summary	Students Listed
Class Periods Listed	Teacher Summary
Department Summary	Teachers Listed
Departments Listed	Yr.-to-Yr. Comparison
District Summary	

In the above example, it is harder for users to find the filters they need, or to even know what filters are available. The expectation that users read the entire filter list to know what is available is impractical. Now consider the exact same filters, which have now been categorized, as shown on the facing page.

Notice how the category labels used there allow the filters to be less wordy (e.g., filters do not have to read *Students Listed, Teachers Listed,* etc. since *Listed* is now already in the category *Names Listed*). Notice how it is easier to know which tests or topics have filters, how users can filter by years of data the reports display, etc.

152

Package/Display Standards: User Interface

Topic or Test	Names Listed
API	Students
Attendance	Programs/Groups
AYP	Class Periods
CAHSEE	Courses
CELDT	Departments
Enrollment (Class Roster)	Teachers
Grades/GPA	Grade Levels
Health	Schools/Sites
STAR (CAPA/CMA/CST/STS)	
Data Summarized For	**Years of Data**
Student	1 Year
Program/Group	2 Years
Class Period	3+ Years
Course	Yr.-to-Yr. Comparison
Department	Cohort Comparison
Teacher	
Grade Level	
School/Site	
District	

Filter categories:

- allow some filter names to be less wordy, reducing clutter;
- make each filter easier to find (and thus make appropriate reports easier to find);
- make it easier for users to know what filters are available;
- save educators time;
- make the report list more user-friendly and thus less intimidating to educators;
- reduce user frustration.

153

Region-Specific

A data system's filters should be based on its region and its reports (their tests/topics, their contents, and their formats). Thus the sample filters on the previous page might not fit the filters and categories best suited to your own clients' data systems. The filter categories used should be the ones that will best organize your users' particular set of report filters, and the report filters used should be the ones that will best apply to your users' particular report types.

Conclusion

Consider which reports are available in your own data system and what your users are most likely to be searching for when they use the data system's filters. This information should clearly correlate with the filters and filter categories available in your data system.

Standard 4.4.03: Consolidate Reports to Support Multiple Inquiries

Consolidate like reports into a single report (which can then be customized by the user with input controls, e.g., selecting a particular test) whenever possible.

One way in which data systems often fail to provide effective navigation is by failing to consolidate reports. For example, many data systems provide a long list of reports that are identical in most ways, with minor variations, and users must wade through this list to find the report they need.

Not only is this arrangement cumbersome to navigate, but it also requires longer processes to flip back and forth between reports during data investigation. Ideally, educators should be able to open a single report type and then use its input controls to select a particular test, group of students, test year, academic year, type of entity to list in the report, etc. Consolidated reports are vital, as they lend the user the power to shape the report to his or her specific needs. They avoid clutter within the report list and interface, and better facilitate recommended approaches to data analysis (discussed later in this chapter).

154

Package/Display Standards: User Interface

Users can still be given the ability to save a particular way they generate a report and share this generation with others. Likewise, a user who filters the report list by a particular test and then opens one of the listed reports can find the report pre-populated with that particular test. However, the data investigation process should not be slowed by an overwhelming list of reports that users must jump in and out of excessively.

Remember Standard 1.1.05 concerning titles (Leave Some Info for the Header and/or Input Controls). Essentially, rather than loading all information into a report's title and thus ending up with a long list of reports users must wade through to find the report they are looking for (and longer processes to flip back and forth between reports during data investigation), let educators open a single report type and then use its input controls to select a particular test, group of students, test year, academic year, type of entity to list in the report, etc.

If the result would be a longer wait time while a report was generated, the DSRP will need to explore possible solutions, as allowed by the technology.

> **Example:** Depending on the technology used, there could be the option of constructing multiple/different reports "behind the scenes" to which different input control selections lead, but to the user the report would still appear to be (i.e., function as, on the front end) a single report. The report can still be set up to run in a default mode based on most popular selections (so users can run the report without thinking of anything if they want to, see what it looks like, and then make changes to how the report is run if needed).

The user can still use test title filters to find reports that can be used to communicate that test's results, and an "*Extended* Report List" can allow users to refer others to more specific, partially generated reports and bookmark them directly for their own use. However, consolidated reports are vital, as they lend the user the power to shape the report to his or her specific needs.

Part of the reason this is ideal relates to clutter (e.g., too much information in titles creates clutter, too many reports on a list of report options creates clutter, etc.). However, a large part of why this is ideal relates to research on the best ways to approach data analysis.

Educators are often trained in a specific approach to data investigation, such as the use of essential questions or data dialogues. Some approaches to analysis involve a combination of strategies, such as Bernhardt's (2004) popular recommendation to identify a problem, then hunches and hypotheses, and then questions before accessing data.

Each of these methods gets at the bigger questions and needs that are driving data investigation. For example, only an educator needing data in order to report it to another (such as for accountability) would simply want to know, "How did my students score on *that test*?" Typically, though an educator might seem driven by this question on the surface, a number or score has little meaning. What the educator really wants to know in this example, based on this test, is something along these lines:

- Did my students perform well?
- Did my students show improvement?
- How did my students perform in relation to my colleagues?
- How did my subgroups of students perform in relation to one another?
- When considered with multiple measures, did the new reading program I am using likely help my students' performance?
- And so on.

Due to the merits of consulting multiple measures, it is not advisable to focus on a single test when using data. Rather, data systems need to allow easy linking of data from different sources, such as from different assessments, reporting of both assessments and non-assessments, and reporting on multiple periods and years to display progress (Dougherty, 2015). Yet many report lists are comprised mainly of single-test reports and often lack reports on non-test data. This single-test emphasis sends the wrong message and hampers good data use.

Thus most data systems' report titles do notoriously little to facilitate recommended data investigation practices. For example, consider how a single reporting investigation can be expressed in three data investigation methods/prompts:

- **Question:** Did I help raise my students' ability to analyze literature last year?
- **Theory:** I helped raise my students' ability to analyze literature last year.
- **Topic:** My students' growth—or lack of growth—in literature analysis last year.

The question, theory, and topic given above constitute a very common reason an educator would want to use a data system and its reports. However, compare that question, theory, and topic to an actual list of report titles in your data system. Is there a clear relationship between the two? The answer is often *no*. Rather, data system reports are often *test*-focused.

The way most data reports are set up, with a different report title (and thus a different report on the report list) for each measure, educators have to go through the following steps whenever they view the results of one measure (e.g., Test A) and want to switch to another measure type (e.g., Portfolio A):

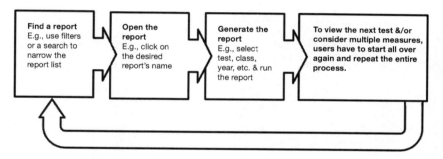

Figure 7.1

Often data inquiries are not linear, and educators must "flip back and forth" between in-depth results. This means leaving one data source's test's (or other measure's) results but then returning to them again to check something when other results trigger a notion. Thus the problem of reports being arranged by test rather than by data inquiry is compounded. If reports are also separated by format (e.g., "Grouped by Course"), the problem is further compounded.

Now consider how the data investigation is improved by consolidating reports and letting users control a report's variations through its input controls:

Package/Display Standards: User Interface

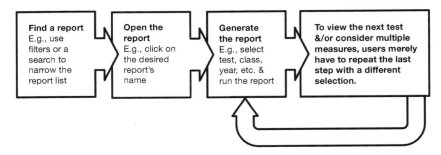

Figure 7.2

Users can still find results for a particular test by filtering the report list by that test. However, once they are viewing one measure's results within a report, they can consider other measures with more ease: either by changing one input control, or by comparing scores from multiple measures within the same report. Of course, reports displaying multiple measures simultaneously should also be available (something covered in the next chapter).

For Those Used to Test-Based Reports

If your reports are test-based, your report list is likely too long for users to skim all report titles looking for tests for which they want to view reports. Thus users are likely using report list filters to find what they need anyway.

Nonetheless, one or more of the following can offer added support to users when you consolidate reports:

- A user who filters the report list by a particular test and then opens one of the listed reports can find the report pre-populated with that particular test's data.

- Users can still be given the ability to save a particular way they generate a report and share this generation with others.

- Users can follow an "Expanded Report List" link to a page where the common, multiple generation formats for each report are listed (and accessible via click).

Package/Display Standards: User Interface

> Change is hard, and many users could prefer test-specific data reports simply because it is what they are used to using. The last bullet above will especially help these users. However, as with any major change in your report environment, you should work with those overseeing user PD and support to ensure a smooth transition.

As detailed in this book's "Label Standards" chapter, a list of twenty test-based (and test-titled) reports could be consolidated into just three reports simply by making "Test Type" and "Group Results By" into input controls. The reports to which these input control selections lead may essentially be different reports (as their columns, headers, etc. might differ from test to test), but an interface that *treats* them as a single report in the user's eyes lends itself better to recommended data use.

Depending on how overtaxed a report's input controls are, the report list types (e.g., site, student, or teacher) could also be handled by input controls to turn the original example of twenty reports (or the three reports they became) into a single report without losing any report options. Even if only *some* report consolidation opportunities are taken, it will likely be an improvement. See "Leave Some Info for the Header and/or Input Controls" in the "Label Standards" chapter and "Facilitate Recommended Data Investigation Practices" later in this chapter for more details.

While the above example was helped by consolidating tests and report formats into fewer reports, the titles remain test-based:

- STAR Scores Site List
- STAR Scores Student List
- STAR Scores Teacher List

Thus the consolidation makes the data system and its reports *better* facilitators of best practices for data investigation (e.g., easier to view multiple tests), but it does not fully solve the problems of:

- reports (and report titles) not being open to non-test measures; and
- reports (and report titles) not matching the types of questions, theories, and topics with which educators are trained to begin data investigations.

159

Package/Display Standards: User Interface

Consolidated Report List

1-to-1 Correlation Identification

1-to-1 Correlation Change

Correlation Identification

Correlation Change Identification

Entity's Measure Focus

Entity's Area Focus

Entity's Measure Breakdown

Multiple Entities' Measure Breakdown

Entity's Multiple Measure Overview

Entity's Multiple Area Overview

Multiple Entities' Measure Comparison

Multiple Entities' Area Comparison

Multiple Entities' Multiple Measure Comparison

Multiple Entities' Multiple Area Comparison

Fit Criteria Identification

Requirement Fulfillment

Entity's Measure Change

Entity's Area Change

Entity's Multiple Measure Change

Entity's Multiple Area Change

Multiple Entities' Measure Change

Multiple Entities' Area Change

Multiple Entities' Multiple Measure Change

Position on Continuum

On the contrary, the Consolidated Report List shown features 24 reports that are not test-based and can be manipulated to (as a whole) suit virtually any data investigation an educator might need to conduct. The "Content Standards" chapter of this book contains more details on these reports in its sample needs matrix, profiling how this suite of reports is arranged effectively by topic to better support recommended data analysis practices. This approach to topic-based reports involves using variables such as test (or other measure) as input controls but also as filters on the report list (so educators can still determine which reports offer access to particular results).

The move to topic-based (as opposed to test-based) reports is recommended. However, if your report environment is not ready to make the move to topic-based reporting, consolidating reports and making better use of reports' input controls can improve your data system in the meantime. This is an important step in the move to better facilitate best practices for data investigation.

Standard 4.4.04: Design Consistency

Remain as consistent as possible from one report to the next in terms of design as long as the design remains well suited to the data's appropriate analysis.

As shared in the online account of all related research, not much has changed over time in terms of evidence of the benefits of remaining as consistent as possible from one report to the next as long as the design is well suited to the data's recommended analysis. When something is unfamiliar to someone, and especially when it is also related to a topic that already intimidates someone (as data and technology can do), that person's emotional filter can go up, making otherwise-understandable concepts harder to comprehend. By giving each report in a data system a similar look and feel, this emotional filter can be diminished. Some examples of report design consistency include:

- reports always read left to right and top to bottom;
- headers always look and act the same;
- the same colors are used to communicate the same meanings.

The need for design consistency is one of many reasons why nearly all of a data system's key reports should be designed simultaneously before reports are built and released to users, as opposed to designing and then building one report at a time (covered in the "Content Standards" chapter for Standard 5.2.02). Imagine if you built a house by designing and building

Package/Display Standards: User Interface

one room at a time: there would be a lot of missed opportunities for the more streamlined design you would have achieved if all rooms had been envisioned ahead of time. The same is true of designing reports one by one rather than mapping a design for all major reports ahead of time. The "Content Standards" chapter covers this concept in detail.

Input Controls

Standard 4.5.01: Facilitate Recommended Data Investigation Practices

Offer input controls that facilitate data investigation practices that are recommended for users. For example, allow educators to open a single report and use its input controls to easily change the measure being viewed, rather than requiring users to select a test-specific report and then return to the report list to find and select another test-specific report in order to investigate multiple measures.

> **Input controls** are the means through which a user communicates selected information to the data system (e.g., a drop-down menu of options).

Input controls allow users to customize the manner in which a report is generated. This allows the same report to serve multiple functions, thus limiting the list of reports to a manageable size. In the examples in the book's eResources, the educator uses the *School* input control to select *N. D. Middle* from the drop-down menu so the *Subgroup Summary* report will display data only from that school.

The need for data system input controls to facilitate recommended data investigation practices was previously discussed in this book ("Leave Some Info for the Header and/or Input Controls" in the "Label Standards" chapter and the Standard 4.4.03 section earlier in this chapter). Here is a recap on key benefits to creating fewer reports with more input control options:

Package/Display Standards: User Interface

- The process of switching back and forth between different test types, reporting groups, etc. is faster, since users do not have to return to the report list and find a new report in order to view the same (or practically same) report with different parameters.

- Recommended data investigation processes (e.g., using essential questions or theory-led data dialogues) are better supported.

- There is no longer disconnect between report titles vs. what educators are hoping to know (e.g., "Did my Filipino kids improve academically as much as my Hispanic kids?" vs. "State Score Report").

- Clutter within each report title is reduced.

- Clutter within the report list is reduced.

- Users are more likely to find what they need.

- The process of finding a specific/needed report is faster.

- Users do not waste time wading through a long report list or repeatedly adding additional filters to make the list more manageable.

- Users are less likely to feel frustrated.

- Thus users are more likely to use the data system again to help students.

- There are fewer reports for you to manage (saving DSRP time and resources).

For reasons discussed, reports' input controls should allow for the number of report generation variations to be extended when reports are consolidated into fewer reports in the user's eyes.

> **Example:** If your report list is long and thus difficult to navigate, you might opt to not have three "3-Yr Growth Summary" reports titled "3-Yr Growth Summary by Course", "3-Yr Growth Summary by Department", and "3-Yr Growth Summary by Period", and to instead provide a single "3-Yr Growth Summary" report, and a "Separate Results By" input control should contain the options of "Course", "Department", and "Period" so the single report (as perceived by the user) can be run in these three different ways.

Input control contents that include options such as these, rather than relegating them to a long list of report titles, can better facilitate recommended data investigation practices for reasons previously discussed.

It can be helpful to provide users access to the more specific reports (e.g., "3-Yr Growth Summary *by Period*") through an "Extended Report List" so they can still refer others to partially generated reports and bookmark them directly for their own use. However, it is vital to recommended data investigation practices to give users access to a report with more flexibility (e.g., "3-Yr Growth Summary"). This flexibility will not require returning to a report list (to find a new report) in order to make a minor variation in how it is generated.

Reports' input controls must be constructed to allow for these variations. Examples of these types of input controls include (* indicates the most common controls):

- **Scope**
  - State
  - Country
  - Similar School
  - District
  - School*
  - Department
  - Course*
  - Teacher*
  - Period
  - Separate Results by
- **Test**
  - Test Year*
  - Test Type
  - Test Subject
  - Test Title*
  - Subgroup Type
  - Show on Report
  - Data Source

- **Students**
  - Academic Year*
  - Grade Level*
  - Program/Group
  - Race/Ethnicity*
  - Language*
  - Special Education Status*
  - Other Filter

Knights et al. (2014) found giving educators the tools needed to explore information resolved issues related to inadequate and inaccessible data. Input controls can be one of the most powerful tools in facilitating good data investigation practices.

Standard 4.5.02: Required Controls Are Visible

If "hiding" some input controls (e.g., to not overwhelm users), do not hide any controls required for the report to generate.

When a single report has a large number of input controls, a data system might "hide" some of the controls (e.g., accessed by an "advanced" link) so it takes an extra click to view and use them. This can help prevent novice users from being intimidated by an overabundance of options, yet still allows advanced users to access and use the additional input controls.

This practice can work as long as all *required* input controls are as immediately and readily available as the core input controls. In other words, if a user must make a selection from the *Test Year* input control in order to successfully generate a report, the *Test Year* input control should not be one of the hidden controls. Otherwise, many users will typically try to generate the report without the hidden controls, get an error message, and possibly be frustrated and/or confused. This can happen to novice users in particular. Even if users are not frustrated and/or confused, this event will waste some of their time, forcing them to take at least two tries (rather than one) to generate a single report.

Standard 4.5.03: Gray-out Unavailable Options and Leave out Never-Available Options

Gray-out unavailable options (e.g., any options for which there *can be* data but there is *not* data are still listed, but in a lighter/gray font). Do not display options that are never available for particular parameters (e.g., grade levels that are not taught at a particular site).

Graying-out unavailable input control options means when users look at a menu of options, any options for which there *can be* data (e.g., at a K-6 school there *can be* data for students in grades Kindergarten through 6) but there is *not* data (e.g., there *can be* Asian kids in a grade level, but there just happen to be no Asian kids in a grade level for a particular school year) are still listed, but in a lighter/gray font. In other words, options that can normally be selected to generate a report but happen not to be available for a report with particular parameters (e.g., a particular school year, another particular demographic, etc.) will not result in a report being successfully generated and thus should be grayed-out. See the example on the facing page.

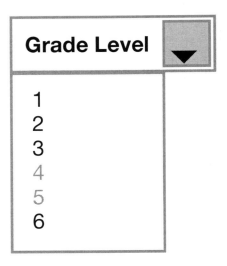

Figure 7.3

Package/Display Standards: User Interface

> **Example:** Imagine you are running a report for Special Ed. students at a school site for the 2012–2013 school year, and you want to run it for each grade level. You would encounter the Grade Level menu (shown here) for a school that serves grades 1–6 but which happens to have no Special Ed. students enrolled in grades 4 or 5. Thus grades 4 and 5 are visible but they are grayed-out and thus cannot be selected.

Graying-out unavailable options allows users to:

- know not to waste their time selecting options that will not successfully render a report (e.g., if I am running a report disaggregated by each race/ethnicity at my school and I see—via grayed-out option—there are no Native Hawaiians/Pacific Islanders at my school, I will not waste my time trying to run the report for Native Hawaiians/Pacific Islanders);

- more easily gain awareness of data issues (e.g., if I am running a report for EL students at a school site but I happen to notice RFEP is grayed-out even though the school has many Redesignated Fluent English Proficient students, I would instantly know there is a problem with the school's RFEP data—such as how students are coded or how data is mapped in the data system/report—even though I was not trying to run a report for RFEP students; fixing this might even fix my EL data, as redesignated students might otherwise have been erroneously counted as EL, which was their previous language proficiency status);

- learn added information about the data (e.g., if I am running a report for the district's GATE students in grade 8 and notice grades 9–12 grayed-out, indicating there are no GATE students in grades 9–12 for a particular school year, I might gain insight into a problem where students were not maintaining their GATE status when they transitioned school levels, encouraging an investigation into why).

Notice the menu shown in the previous example does not bother showing grade K or grades 7–12 at all. This is because this particular school site never has students enrolled in those grades. Options that are never available for particular parameters (e.g., grade levels for a particular site,

167

Package/Display Standards: User Interface

class names within a particular department, etc.) should never be featured among input control options, as they will only add clutter and confuse users.

Conflicting Arguments

If a particular data system's structure/technology does not allow for this standard to be implemented without dramatically slowing the time it takes for input controls to load (and thus a report to be generated), you should consider forgoing the standard, but not without:

- spending time thinking hard and creatively before concluding a win–win solution (e.g., grayed-out input control options and fast report generation time) is not possible, and trying to find a way to make it work;
- weighing the pros and cons of including the feature (e.g., grayed-out input control options) vs. not including the feature, and selecting the best option "for now" while also planning for a more ideal solution in the future if a compromise must be struck in the meantime.

Standard 4.5.04: Categorized Control Display

Display/group input controls by category (e.g., by *Scope*, *Test*, and *Students*).

Imagine a grocery store where aisles were not devoted to specific purposes. You would not see an aisle for snacks, another aisle for cleaning and paper goods, another aisle for medicine and hygiene products, another aisle for bread and baked goods, and so on. You would have a difficult time finding and selecting the paper towels you ran into the store to buy if all product categories were jumbled together.

The same is true of input controls. Like filters used to make a data system's report list more manageable, categorizing input controls (e.g., by *Scope*, *Test*, and *Students*, as shown in Figure 7.4) can help users run a report faster, easier, and with more confidence. In addition, categorizing input controls allows the data system to communicate more easily. And the data system *should* communicate any selection requirements so users do not struggle with controls.

Package/Display Standards: User Interface

Example I

- Sets of controls that must be selected in different ways (e.g., in the "Must Select Students . . ." set users can select controls in any order, but in the "Get as Specific as You Want" and "Must Select a 'Test'" sets users have to make selections top-to-bottom because the option they select for one input control populates which options are available for another input control).

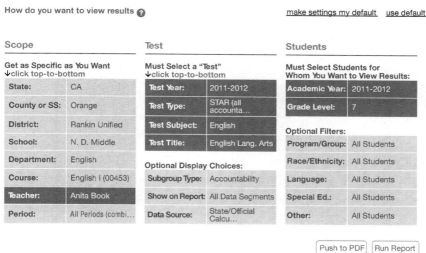

Figure 7.4

- Sets of controls that are optional vs. required (e.g., in each optional set users can use any controls they want or none at all, but in the "Must Select Students . . ." set users have to make selections for all available input controls or else a report won't generate).

Categorizing controls makes it easier to communicate these requirements in a way that is not repetitive and thus does not contribute to clutter. The next section will demonstrate how sample input controls (shown above) can function.

169

Package/Display Standards: User Interface

Standard 4.5.05: Time-Saving Options

Offer time-saving options such as: (a) easy disaggregation of data; (b) easy aggregation (e.g., among single grade-level options, let users opt to select *All Tested (combined)* for *Grade Level* to generate a single report in which all grade levels' results are consolidated/summarized); (c) run multiple reports at once (e.g., let users opt to select *Each Tested (separate)* for *Grade Level* to generate a separate report for each grade level within a single generation so the user does not have to run each report separately); (d) data source options (e.g., using state/official data source files vs. the data system's local/roster-based data); and (e) multi-select (e.g., let users opt to select multiple options simultaneously on a single drop-down menu).

Each input control is a chance to make busy educators' jobs easier. Notice the varied input control options and consider how some of these time-saving options might work well (and be possible) in your data system:

Easy Disaggregation

When viewing a report, users should be able to easily disaggregate the data. This means they should easily be able to narrow down the report's focus to include only a portion of the data it is capable of encompassing.

> **Example:** After **running** a report to show all of my Period 1's students' scores on *Test A*, I can select "Hispanic" on the "Subgroup" input control so the report will now behave as if only the Hispanic students in my class exist (e.g., instead of showing the scores of all 35 Period 1 students, the report will now only show the scores of the six Hispanic students I have in Period 1, while also summarizing the performance of all Hispanic students).

Package/Display Standards: User Interface

Easy Aggregation

An upcoming example shows how selecting All Tested (combined) for Grade Level would automatically generate a single report in which all grade levels' results are consolidated/summarized. This provides users with quick answers and further avoids the need for mental arithmetic, as cautioned against in Standard 4.2.02.

> **Example:** Some **accountability** models are based on how school sites performed overall (i.e., all tested grades combined). Thus running a report to quickly judge how many of a school site's students—all grades combined—reached proficiency would be valuable.

Sample input control options that also allow for easy aggregation:

- Scope:
  - When the user clicks *School* in Example I (in color online), one of the options (listed along with individual schools) is ***All Schools***. The report then groups all schools' results together (as opposed to reporting on each school individually).
  - When the user clicks *Department* in Example I, one of the options (listed along with individual departments) is ***All Departments***.
  - When the user clicks *Course* in Example I, one of the options (listed along with individual courses) is ***All Courses***.
- Test:
  - When the user clicks *Test Type* in Example I, one of the options (listed along with individual test types) is ***STAR (all accountability combined)***, which groups results of all tests within this single testing program related to accountability.
- Students:
  - When the user clicks *Grade Level* in Example I, one of the options (listed along with individual grade levels) is ***All Tested (combined)***.

Each of these options would appear at the top of drop-down menus so they would not be missed and can also serve as the control's defaults.

171

Multiple Reports Run at Once

In the example above, notice input control options that save report-generating time.

> **Example:** Selecting *Each Tested (separate)* for *Grade Level* automatically generates a separate report for each grade level so the user does not have to run each report separately. For a PK-12 district, this would allow a district or site administrator to generate 14 separate reports in the same time it takes to run one.

Sample input control options that also allow users to run multiple reports at once:

- Scope:
  - When the user clicks *School* in Example I, one of the options (listed along with individual schools) is **Each School (separated)**. The report then features each school's report. A district administrator might run this in order to give each principal his or her own school's report at an upcoming principals' meeting.
  - When the user clicks *Department* in Example I, one of the options (listed along with individual departments) is **Each Department (separated)**.
  - When the user clicks *Course* in Example I, one of the options (listed along with individual courses) is **Each Course (separated)**.
- Students:
  - When the user clicks *Grade Level* in Example I, one of the options (listed along with individual grade levels) is **Each Tested (separated)**.

Each of these options would appear near the top of drop-down menus so they would not be missed.

Package/Display Standards: User Interface

Data Source Options

When running reports to judge whether accountability criteria were met or to display data that will be shared with the public, it can be very helpful to run reports that use state/official data source files (rather than the data system's local/roster-based data) so numbers match "official" data used by government agencies and available to the general public online.

Factors such as student mobility and scheduling changes can cause differences between reports run with state/official data source files and reports run with the data system's local/roster-based data files. Giving users the option of picking which data source they would like to use can save them time, trouble, and confusion. Since such a selection completely impacts how the report's data is run, separate reports with data mapped in these two different ways can exist "behind the scenes" so users retain the experience of working with a single report that has both of these options.

Multi-Select

Allowing users to select multiple options on a drop-down menu allows them to further customize reports to meet their specific needs and can also save paper and streamline analyses by allowing users to bypass some features. For example, a user might select both Performance Level and Performance Level Distribution for Show on Report, yet bypass other available sections the user did not want displayed on the report.

Conclusion

Consider whether or not some of the above input control options might work well (and be possible) in your data system. If some are not possible or (based on how the data system is set up) will cause negative repercussions that outweigh the benefits, forgo the options but do not forget them. Technology and data systems are constantly evolving, and many worthwhile features that are currently possible and featured in data systems were not so easily achieved (if at all) a number of years ago. Remember the benefits of these options so you can implement them as soon as it is feasible for your particular situation.

Package/Display Standards: User Interface

References

Bernhardt, V. L. (2004). *Data analysis for continuous school improvement.* Larchmont, NY: Eye on Education.

Dougherty, C. (2015). *How school district leaders can support the use of data to improve teaching and learning.* Act, Inc. Retrieved from www.act.org/research/policymakers/pdf/Use-of-Data.pdf (accessed Ocotber 30, 2015).

Knights, G., Allee, W., & Center, B. (2014). *Developing decision-driving data displays: A case study at Newport-Mesa Unified School District.* California Educational Research Association (CERA) Conference. Presentation conducted from Paradise Point Resort, San Diego, CA.

Outing, S., & Ruel, L. (2006, January 30). The best of Eyetrack III: What we saw when we looked through their eyes. *Eyetrack III,* 1–9. The Poynter Institute. Retrieved from www.academia.edu/546755/The_best_of_eyetrack_III_What_we_saw_when_we_looked_through_their_eyes (accessed October 30, 2015).

SAS Institute (2013). *Best practices in information management, reporting and analytics for education.* Retrieved from https://fs24.formsite.com/edweek/form15/secure_index.html (accessed October 30, 2015).

8 | Content Standards

Definition of Content

The content of each data report and the report suite as a whole all need to cover key educator data needs in an efficient manner. Data system reporting content consists of:

- what you get within each report once the reports are opened;
- the report offering as a whole (i.e., the suite of reports).

Great labeling, supplemental documentation, help system support, and an effective package/display will be useless in helping educators and their students if the data reporting *content* does not do what educators need it to do.

Returning to our medical analogy, we can see how effective content is vital to an over-the-counter product's success. If a "cold remedy" really contained nothing but sugar and food coloring, it would not help cure a cold. A product is useless—no matter how well you package it or embed support for its use—if the product's content does not do what users need it to do. For example, if someone buys a product to stop a fever, the product should stop a fever. The product may have multiple uses, but these uses are usually specific and not overly numerous. Also, expired medications are removed from shelves so as not to poison users. Thus over-the-counter product content remains effective. The same is true of data reports and data systems.

To be "over-the-counter" and thus easy to use, each report's content should be appropriate for intended audiences, and "expiration" should be

Content Standards

considered (e.g., calculations and textual guidance such as footers should be kept current with changing legislation and user needs). Likewise, the *suite* of reports should be a streamlined collection that covers all key needs without overwhelming users.

How to Implement Effective Content

Resources

Access the following:

- OTCD *Content* standards (on pages 11–12 of OTCD Standards)
- Details on research-based evidence supporting OTCD *Content* standards

An ideal data reporting environment should reflect the OTCD *Content* standards, which stipulate research-based ways data systems/reports can feature effective content. These standards can be found online with details on the extensive research informing every standard. The rest of this chapter contains a lesson on how to implement each OTCD *Content* standard.

Real-World Implementation: Content

By Leo Bialis-White, Vice President of Impact, Schoolzilla

At Schoolzilla, we build and help others build visualizations to support data conversations at schools. To do this, our report content needs four qualities:

- Timely
- Complete
- Accurate
- Explorable

176

At Schoolzilla, timely is achieved by having a cloud-based solution that refreshes data as frequently as end-users (e.g., principals and teachers) need it. Complete requires pulling data from multiple sources for a comprehensive view of an organization, classroom, or student. Accuracy is a collaborative process that necessitates data quality reports to illuminate errors and processes/structures to improve the data quality. Finally, we create and co-create explorable visualizations where users can quickly identify high-level trends and drill down into more detail to answer additional hypotheses (at Schoolzilla, we use Tableau as our business intelligence tool).

Importantly, the development of timely, complete, accurate, and explorable reports requires adherence to Rankin's standards of content. Our development process—inspired by Stanford's Design School—includes multiple cycles (OTCD Standard 5.2.02) with a range of end-users in multiple different settings, which helps identify and clarify the key use cases and questions to be answered (5.2.04). Reports and reports playlists are audience-specific (5.1.02); for example, cross-school comparisons in college-readiness are most appropriate for school leaders and superintendents. The playlists are also designed to provide a digestible amount of reports and insights (5.2.03), so end-users can quickly glean the insights they need to inform their data-driven conversations.

Each Report

Standard 5.1.01: Expiration

Keep report contents current, e.g., with changing: (a) legislation (e.g., accountability requirements, retention criteria, terminology used, etc.); (b) user needs (e.g., growing term familiarity); (c) research developments such as those concerning users' data needs (e.g., new approaches to data use); and (d) technology developments (e.g., if reports cannot accommodate drill-down capabilities when needed, the report environment is dated).

Medicine is removed from drugstore shelves as it expires. To not keep the over-the-counter offering up to date would be dangerous for consumers and highly negligent of those providing the products. The same is true of data systems in terms of report contents staying up to date. If outdated data report contents are used to treat the needs of students, they can lead to flawed conclusions and flawed data-informed decisions, which can hurt students.

Legislation

Reports should reflect the latest legislation. In some cases this will be on a report-by-report basis, as some reports from previous years might need to retain configurations based on outdated legislation (e.g., calculations or criteria specific to that testing year), whereas new years' reports will certainly need to be updated.

Examples of report aspects that can "expire" in terms of legislation and thus require change include (but are not limited to) those relating to:

- Accountability (requirements, components, etc.)
- Tests (those used, the way they are reported, levels tested, etc.)
- Criteria (graduation, retention, status, redesignation, etc.)
- Demographics (name, definition, qualifying criteria, etc.)
- Calculations (data included, subject weights, etc.)

When report aspects expire, this can require change within other reporting components.

> **Example:** If a state changed how *Proficiency* was calculated on its English Language proficiency exam for EL students, the reporting environ-ment would need to update all areas explaining this calculation, such as a report's footer (Label), reference sheet and reference guide (Supplemental Documentation), and data analysis lessons (Help System).

It might also have to change how *Proficiency* is displayed on reports (Package/Display), such as which scores are displayed in red vs. green.

If the new calculation requires different criteria than before (such as the consideration of number of days the student has lived in the U.S.), the reporting environment might also have to change what data is contained in reports (Content).

Other Types of Expiration

Each report's content must also remain current with users' changing needs (e.g., growing term familiarity), research developments (e.g., newly identified "at risk" indicators), users' data needs (e.g., new approaches to data use), and technology developments (e.g., if reports cannot accommodate drill-down capabilities when needed, the report environ-ment is dated). These changes all relate to keeping up with changing times, and some specific examples are provided later in this chapter.

Standard 5.1.02: Audience-Appropriate

Cater design contents to the report's predetermined audience(s) in terms of its: (a) knowledge and skills (e.g., terms and explanations); (b) role and how it will use the report (e.g., components included vs. excluded); and (c) region (e.g., format that best accommodates an assessment's reporting guidelines).

In addition to matching a report's label, supplemental documentation, and package/display to the audience for which it is designed and allowing for varied audience needs in the help system, a report's content should also be designed around its predetermined audience. Even when users are all educators, these users can still vary widely in terms of:

- knowledge and skills (which are influenced by background, confidence levels, and emotional reactions to reports);
- role;
- ways report will be used;
- region;
- and so on.

Content Standards

These audience differences can warrant special consideration for report aspects such as:

- terms used and/or defined;

- explanations provided;

- components excluded vs. included;

- report format to accommodate region-specific assessment's reporting requirements;

- and so on.

In fact, many of the above decisions (and more) made when determining a report's content are informed by the audience's region.

Remember the research concerning the need to avoid information-overload. Note the relative consistency among evidence (even over time) concerning the dangers of jargon. Just as you keep a report's audience in mind when implementing other OTCD Standards, do the same for a report's content.

Report Suite

Standard 5.2.01: Expiration

Keep the report suite current, e.g., with changing: (a) legislation (e.g., reports addressing new forms of accountability); (b) user needs (e.g., sync with new edtech); (c) research developments such as those concerning users' data needs (e.g., the system is dated if every educator does not have access to timely data or if no reports are predictive or show progress over time); and (d) technology developments (e.g., the system is dated if students are not tied to unique identifiers or if data is not appropriately collected, stored, and protected).

The possibilities for reporting environments such as data systems are endless. A good reporting environment is one that does not surrender to complacency, but rather constantly reflects a "we can always get better" mindset of the team behind it. In addition to improvements based on this mindset, other improvements to the report suite will be necessitated by changing times.

The future is always on its way. Times will change. These will always be on the education horizon:

- new standards;

- new demands and accountability models;

- new assessments;

- new research;

- new technologies;

- new teaching trends;

- new analysis trends;

- and so on.

These will typically be good things, because they will have added history and research to inform them. Ideally, they will build on what came before them with the goal of helping us help students even more.

Legislation-based changes were covered extensively in the "Each Report" section of this chapter (e.g., for Standard 5.1.01), so please see that section for legislation specifics. Changes warranted by user needs, research developments, and technology developments will be covered more extensively here. For report suites keeping ahead of these changes, this can mean such enhancements as:

- Allowing a question- or theory-based search to render a report generated in a way that specifically addresses the question or theory that was posed. One individual report would not be built for each individual question or theory; rather, topic-based reports would be generated/customized to match the question or theory posed.

- Providing an expressed question with its exact answer(s). This is similar to the above notion, but the answer would be explicitly stated for the user.

- Integrating reports with results- and audience-based professional learning models, curriculum, and other tools specifically designed to remedy any issues indicated by the data. For example, a school district in Fairfax County, Virginia, that serves approximately 184,000 students, hopes to someday enhance its curriculum and assessment resource system so that it makes data-informed intervention recommendations to teachers (Davis, 2013).

- Extensive (as opposed to no or minimal) predictive analytics. Consider this: when students at Purdue University took at least two courses that used the university's data mining and analysis software, which provided both teachers and students with data-informed feedback on *risk* of poor student performance, graduation rates were 21.48 percent higher (Tally, 2013).

The key is to use the growing wealth of knowledge and resources to keep the data system most supportive of the evolving needs of its users and evolving research developments, as well as the evolving technology developments that allow report suites to get even better at what they are designed to do.

Standard 5.2.02: Proactive Design Approach (Preplanned, Centralized)

Utilize a predominantly proactive (rather than reactive) design model for report development and maintenance where the core suite of reports is preplanned in a centralized fashion (e.g., someone with an education/ data/design background should lead the project, solicit feedback, etc.).

It would be fruitless to discuss building a suite of reports that adheres to this book's standards without addressing the processes and structures through which they are built. This is because the processes and structures through which they are designed and created have an immense impact on the report suite's success.

Factors that Drive Successful Report Suite Design

Many factors can influence your success when seeking to improve your reporting environment by implementing the OTCD Standards in this book.

Content Standards

Three characteristics stand out as being particularly important yet sometimes evasive:

- proactive design model;
- positive mindset;
- "lean in" culture.

OTCD can still be implemented in their absence, but the process will likely be undermined, taking longer and/or never reaching the same level of completion/ quality that could have been achieved if the characteristics in this section were adopted by stakeholders involved in the data system's improvement. A proactive design model, positive mindset, and a "lean in" culture can all help to drive OTCD implementation.

Proactive Design Model (Preplanned and Centralized)

Report development and maintenance should assume a proactive—rather than reactive—design model. This necessity relates to whoever is planning the suite of reports, and thus the DSRP can be any of the following:

- an educator or educator team at districts where the district provides its own data system and/or report suite;
- an educator or educator team at districts where an outside vendor provides the district's data system and/or report suite, and educators supplement the report suite with reports they create;
- an outside vendor rather than an educator.

Again, the processes and structures through which data systems are designed and created have an immense impact on the success of the system's reporting environment. Consider these questions:

> Have your users ever requested a report or report enhancement from you, and you agree it is a good idea, but it cannot be done anytime soon because your report builder is "super busy"?

183

Content Standards

> . . . or have your users not made any such requests, yet your clients find your data system report suite does not cover all of their key needs?

No data reporting product is without enhancement requests, but the above problems often occur when a data system has ineffective processes and structures through which reports are designed and created. Many DSRPs are designing, building, and deploying reports one by one in a reactive model driven by client/educator requests. While it is vital to listen to users and to respond to their needs, the client-*driven* (rather than client-*informed*) approach to report building is less equipped to improve educators' data analysis problems.

In addition, there are reasons why a *reactive* model is inherently flawed (and thus a model that is both client driven *and* reactive is doubly cursed). Consider the following diagram, which compares two different report suite design approaches.

Imagine a cook at a restaurant where no menu was planned ahead of time, and where anyone orders anything he or she wants, and the cook considers individually if such a meal would be good.

- Imagine how busy and crazed the cook would be, constantly scrambling to accommodate the new meals and factor them into the rest of the menu without letting any of the other meal preparations slip.
- Imagine how busy and crazed the restaurant's staff would be as they fielded customer requests and complaints.
- Finally, imagine how crazy the menu (and thus the customer's experience) would be if this reactive approach were the manner in which the menu was built, rather than planning a balanced menu ahead of time with a selection of desserts to account for all tastes, a selection of appetizers to account for all tastes, and so on.

The result would be an extremely long, unbalanced menu, and it would be hard for users to find what they needed in all that clutter and chaos.

Likewise, it is no wonder a report programmer is busy and overwhelmed when such a reactive approach is used for building and maintaining a report suite. Sadly, the worse consequence is the reduced quality in the reports and in the reporting suite as a whole.

184

Reactive Approach (akin to drawing up architectural plans and then building a single room for a house, then drawing up plans and building the next room, etc., without drawing up plans ahead of time for the entire house).

Little Time
DSRP does not pre-plan with mockups for entire suite of key reports that will need to be built to cover all key ed. needs.

Same Time as Below
DSRP builds each report in reaction to educator requests without having, consulting, or integrating with a pre-planned suite of all key reports that are being built. E.g., DSRP might create & reference only a mockup for the single report being built.

Too Much Time
Complaints & requests for changes to the reports come in from educators & from DSRP staff interacting with educators. DSRP fields requests & likely makes changes to reports, but making time for these changes undermines time DSRP needs to build new/remaining reports. There is still no pre-planned suite of key reports, & there is confusion regarding which requests should be honored vs. which are merely the result of educators searching for ways to compensate for inadequate report suite.

Outcome
An ineffective suite of reports: gaps in some areas, overlap in other areas, more educator complaints and frustration, fragmented collection of feedback, overage of reports to manage, clutter, DSRP time spent fixing rather than progressing, etc.

Proactive Approach (akin to drawing up architectural plans for the entire house ahead of time, then making educated adjustments to the house plans only if necessary as each room is built).

Planning Time
DSRP reporting expert creates mockups for entire, cohesive suite of key reports that will be built to cover all key ed. needs. Feedback is collected (from ed. & other DSRP). Suite is compared to an educator needs matrix to avoid gaps & reduce overlap.

Same Time as Above
DSRP builds each report based on the pre-planned suite of all key reports that are being built. As ed. report requests come in during development, mockups of not-yet-built reports are shown to ed. ("Will this suffice?") and revised if necessary.

Little Time
There will be a reduced # of requests to field, so time can be spent on progressing (e.g., keeping up-to-date with data trends).

Outcome
An effective suite of reports: few or no gaps, reduced overlap, happy educators with a clear picture of how things work, happy DSRP staff with a clear plan & clear communication, fewer complaints, fewer reports to manage, less clutter, time spent progressing rather than fixing, better product, better impact on students, etc.

Figure 8.1 Two Different DSRP Approaches to Building Data Report Suites (with Time Spent on Each Stage)

Imagine building a report suite as akin to building a house. A report suite must accommodate all of users' key needs in a way that is easy to live with, just as a comfortable home must do this for its residents. Think of a DSRP that builds reports in a reactive manner as akin to a house builder who draws up architectural plans and then builds a single room for a house, then draws up plans and builds the next room, and so on, without drawing up plans ahead of time for the entire house. Conversely, imagine the benefits of a DSRP that designs most of its suite of reports ahead of time. This is like a house builder who draws up architectural plans for the entire house ahead of time, then makes educated adjustments to the house plans only if necessary as each room is built.

There is a reason most houses are built from architectural plans in which the entire house has been designed. Sure, the homeowner might want to add an addition down the line or remodel a room in the future, but building the house from complete plans would render such changes more minimal. Having a plan ahead of time results in a better planned house, rooms that work well together to meet all of the residents' needs, the reduction of unnecessary repetition (e.g., three kitchens that work in slightly different ways but none of which meets all of the homeowner's needs), etc.

The same is true of data reporting environments and the need to design the core report suite ahead of time. Study Figure 8.1 and the outcomes for each model, which illustrate some of the reasons why planning a report suite ahead of time is vital. Likewise, note how a DSRP reporting expert designs the reports and how educator/client feedback is integrated as a vital component, including prior to report construction. Thus educator/client input is still involved, but a single staff member with educator experience is overseeing the project and the DSRP is mostly planning rather than mostly reacting.

To say, "we do not have *time* to plan the core report suite ahead of time" is like saying, "we do not have *time* to look at a map before navigating our way across the continent." A centralized, preplanned approach will save report creators' time while simultaneously rendering a product more adept at helping educators and students.

Positive Mindset

This book will help most if everyone involved (educator and DSRP, whether the DSRP is educator-comprised or not) maintains proactive mindsets. Frustrations and negativity can undermine OTCD Standards' implementa-tion if left unchecked. If you run into dilemmas, the "Dilemma Countered by Proactive Mindset Table" guidelines can help.

"Lean In" Culture

It might seem odd to cover the topic of gender equality in an edtech book, but navigating gender issues is a crucial component to proactive and successful edtech design. Read more about this topic in the "Work with Educators" chapter of this book.

Conclusion

At the crux of this chapter is a message that also appears throughout the book: the need to work together. In an issue brief on using educational data mining and analytics to improve teaching and learning, the U.S. Department of Education Office of Educational Technology (2012):

- called for better collaboration between the research, commercial, and educational communities in order to co-design the best educational technology tools;
- called on educators to ask critical questions about commercial offerings and purchase intelligently in order to create demand for the most useful educational technology features and uses;
- called on researchers and technology developers to conduct research concerning the effectiveness and usability of data displays.

None of this can be achieved—nor can its benefits—without a proactive, preplanned, centralized design approach involving all stakeholders working together for the common good. We are all in this together, and input from all of us is needed to refine tools that can best help students.

Content Standards

Standard 5.2.03: Not Too Many

Do not offer so many separate reports that the report list is overwhelming and individual reports are hard to find. Instead, plan a report suite that is efficient. For example, each report should accommodate multiple variables as options (such as an input control with multiple measures) and each report's topic should address multiple theories and questions (which can be infinite).

Lots of Data

Consider the "Sample Data Types to Support Educators' Data Analyses" file. This table is meant to provide a sample of the types of data, collected by and for various entities, that can be housed in a data system, reported on in aggregated and disaggregated formats, and used for data-informed decision-making.

While the table contains 333 data *types*, which indicate even more actual *pieces* of data, this list is not exhaustive. There are even more data types—topics about which you can survey, facts you can collect on enrollment forms, etc.—that are likely to help educators make decisions to ultimately help students.

Nonetheless, this data table is thorough in communicating the variety of data that can be helpful. In fact, if you study the list, you will likely think of questions, theories, or topics that could drive data investigations you had not thought of before (e.g., "Is a teacher's sense of belonging (e.g., collegiality) possibly impacting his or her use of the school's official pacing guides?").

Unfortunately, many of these data types are not utilized in educators' data investigations. For example, student and parent survey data is often not collected or integrated into the data system and its reports, or data from different sources is not examined together (finding correlations, etc.). Reasons include:

- The data system cannot house the data type.
- The data system can house the data type, but it was not collected by education staff.

Content Standards

- There are not easy-to-access and -use reports within the data system that communicate the data type in a meaningful way.

- There *are* reports in the data system that communicate the data type in a meaningful way, but they (e.g., their value or applications) are overlooked by educators.

Often the reason is a combination of the middle two bullets: the data system *can* house the data type, but it was not collected by education staff *because* there are not easy-to-access and -use reports within the data system that communicate the data type in a meaningful way. Thus educators are right in asking, "What would be the point collecting and entering data we can't use?" Busy educators are hardly likely to collect data they will never be able to report on and analyze with ease. Their time is better spent on endeavors with potential to make a difference in students' lives.

Thus many valuable questions educators might wonder (e.g., "What characteristics of our 7th and 8th grade students are likely to indicate they will not graduate from high school after they transition from our school?") are left by the wayside when educators use their data system, because their data system does not make answering these questions easy. Rather, educators focus on questions they feel they have a pretty good shot at finding answers to in their data systems. This is part of a dilemma discussed below.

Lots of Questions/Theories/Topics

What is left when educators discard some questions in favor of only those the data system can answer is captured in the questions within "Sample Questions Data Can Help Answer". Granted, the majority of data systems are not able to easily answer most of the questions on this table, meaning educators' lists of questions, theories, or topics begging data investigation have to be reduced even further.

Thus if you compare these questions ("Sample Questions Data Can Help Answer") to the data types ("Sample Data Types to Support Educators' Data Analyses"), you will notice the questions table does not address many of the topics varied datasets have the potential to help answer, even though the questions table contains 183 questions (more questions than most report suites can easily answer).

189

Whole books are written about the infinite number of questions/theories/topics educators can pursue in data investigations that have the potential to ultimately help students. This is also part of a dilemma discussed below.

Dilemma

Considering there are so many types and pieces of data, and so many questions/theories/topics educators want to address with data-informed decision-making, a conundrum might now be brewing in your mind. Do not feel bad if the dilemma even stresses you out, makes you feel defeated, or draws to mind the oft-used term, "drowning in data." Those reactions are common and normal, because the challenge is a substantial one:

> How can a data system's reports address all of educators' key questions/theories/topics, and how can it do so in a way that is user-friendly and not overwhelming?

This chapter's next section, below, is designed to provide answers.

Do Not Create a Separate Report for Every Question/Theory, Though Specific Questions/Theories Can Lead to Appropriate Reports

Housing too many different reports in a data system will make each report harder to find, which will cost educators time and raise frustration levels. Educators and the students they serve cannot benefit from a report if the educator can never find it or gives up on using the data system altogether due to frustration. Thus, trying to craft a single report for every question/theory/topic a data-informed educator could have is not recommended (but keep reading for ways to work with questions and theories).

Titling reports by questions or theories does not work for this very reason. Even though good reports are designed with a specific set of specific functions in mind, the questions and theories educators could address with such a report remain infinite. Consider the **Example** J report

Content Standards

segment (in color online). This is just a *single segment* of the report, and very simplified at that. Yet consider the questions and theories this single graph could be used to address in regards to two administrations of a benchmark assessment used:

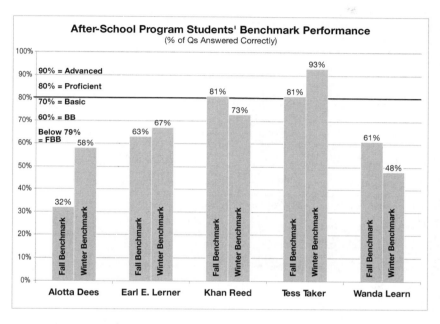

Figure 8.2 Sample Report Segment

As the last row in Table 8.1 implies, the number of questions and theories a report can help answer—even when it is a relatively simple report—is virtually infinite. Likewise, no one can know the verbiage an educator is going to use when couching his or her question or theory.

Also, each educator will likely have multiple questions and theories in need of investigation when approaching even a single report, as Table 8.1 shows reports can address multiple questions and theories. In addition, some educators struggle with finding appropriate questions. For example, when using a data system, most case study teachers struggled when trying to pose questions that could be investigated within the data system to identify areas for improvement (USDEOPEPD, 2011).

Content Standards

Table 8.1 Questions vs. Theories

Sample Question (According to 2 Benchmark Administrations . . .)	Sample Theory (According to 2 Benchmark Administrations . . .)
Who is my highest-performing student?	Tess is my highest-performing student.
Who was my highest-performing student in the fall?	Khan and Tess were my highest-performing students in the fall.
Did my highest-performing student change between fall and winter?	My highest-performing student changed slightly between fall and winter.
Who is my lowest-performing student?	Wanda is my lowest-performing student.
Who was my lowest-performing student in the fall?	Alotta was my lowest-performing student in the fall.
Are most of my students *Proficient?*	Most of my students are not *Proficient.*
Were most of my students *Proficient* in the fall?	Most of my students were not *Proficient* in the fall.
Which students are *Proficient?*	Tess is *Proficient.*
Are more students *Proficient* in the winter than were in the fall?	No more students are *Proficient* in the winter than were in the fall.
Might the supplemental materials I used with Tess but not Khan have had a positive impact?	The supplemental materials I used with Tess but not Khan had a positive impact.
Was the extra 1-on-1 time I spent with Khan and Wanda possibly effective?	The extra 1-on-1 time I spent with Khan and Wanda was not effective.
Might Alotta's frequent absences have had a negative impact on her mastery of standards taught?	Alotta's frequent absences might have had a negative impact on her mastery of standards taught.
Might Wanda's failure to do homework have had a negative impact on her mastery of standards taught?	Wanda's failure to do homework might have had a negative impact on her mastery of standards taught.
Might Alotta's, Earl's, and Tess's added time in the online instructional portal have had a positive impact on their mastery of standards taught?	Alotta's, Earl's, and Tess's added time in the online instructional portal might have had a positive impact on their mastery of standards taught.

Content Standards

Table 8.1 continued

Are most of my students who aren't *Proficient* in the next performance level down (*Basic*)?	Most of my students who aren't *Proficient* are not in the next performance level down (*Basic*).
Which performance level are most students obtaining?	FBB is the performance level most students are obtaining, but only slightly.
Which performance level were most students obtaining in the fall?	BB was the performance level most students were obtaining in the fall, but only slightly.
How many students dropped 1 performance level between fall and winter?	2 students dropped 1 performance level between fall and winter.
Which students dropped 1 performance level between fall and winter?	Khan and Wanda dropped 1 performance level between fall and winter.
How many students jumped multiple performance levels between fall and winter?	0 students jumped multiple performance levels between fall and winter.
Which students jumped multiple performance levels between fall and winter?	Alotta jumped multiple performance levels between fall and winter (false).
How many students dropped multiple performance levels between fall and winter?	0 students dropped multiple performance levels between fall and winter.
Which students dropped multiple performance levels between fall and winter?	Wanda dropped multiple performance levels between fall and winter (false).
Did my lowest-performing student change between fall and winter?	My lowest-performing student changed between fall and winter.
Did most of my students improve between fall and winter?	Most of my students improved between fall and winter.
Was the average amount gained by students who improved more than the average amount decreased by students who dropped?	The average amount gained by students who improved was more than the average amount decreased by students who dropped.

193

Content Standards

Table 8.1 continued

Which students were *Proficient* in the fall?	Khan and Tess were *Proficient* in the fall.
Which students are not *Proficient?*	Alotta, Earl, Khan, and Wanda are not *Proficient.*
Which students were not *Proficient* in the fall?	Alotta, Earl, and Wanda were not *Proficient* in the fall.
How many students jumped 1 performance level between fall and winter?	1 student jumped 1 performance level between fall and winter.
Which students jumped 1 performance level between fall and winter?	Tess jumped 1 performance level between fall and winter.
Etc.	Etc.

Thus a conclusion can be drawn: a data system should not try to tie each report to a single question or theory. This means a question or theory should not be used as a report title.

This moves us to another question:

How *should* reports be organized and titled?

The answer is *by topic*. Topic-titled reports and their organization are covered in the next section.

You might rightfully be thinking, "Wait a second! This book references the abundance of literature encouraging educators to begin data investigations with a question or theory, and this book notes the data system should be structured to support such practices." Since questions and theories are infinite, organizing reports around *topics* offers a manageable system of reports that can still be used to address the abundance of questions and theories.

While it is ill-advised to title each report by question or theory (and thus tie each report to a single question or theory), it is a wonderful thing when data systems allow educators to pick or type a question or theory, which then leads them to a report appropriate for addressing that question or theory (and if input controls are automatically adjusted to best suit the question or theory, so much the better).

194

> **Example:** Imagine your data system allows users to ask a specific question or pose a specific theory—e.g., pick a topic, select a question or theory formula ("How does/did _ affect or correlate with _?"), and use drop-down menus to fill in the blanks. The user could then get a specific answer accompanied and illustrated by an appropriate report.

While organizing/titling reports by question/theory does not work well, allowing users to work with specific questions and theories *within* a data system is ideal and manageable. In addition, Kenny (2010) found turning information the user selected for analysis into words, accompanied by tables and figures, significantly improved the user's data analysis accuracy.

If you are able to accomplish this in your data system, go for it! The series-of-links approach described in the above example, as well as the "Sample Questions Data Can Help Answer" table, can give you some guidance.

Standard 5.2.04: Organized to Cover Needs Matrix

Offer a suite of reports that, as a whole, meets users' key data needs (as organized within a comprehensive needs matrix) in a way that is user-friendly and unintimidating. For example, the suite: (a) has no gaps (gaps occur when key analyses are not facilitated by any of a data system's reports, or when key analyses can only be accommodated when data system reports and/or features not intended for those analyses have to be used in a cumbersome way because no better alternatives exist in the data system); (b) is topic-focused (whereas theories and questions are infinite); and (c) is region-specific.

Results from a Lexia Learning survey of more than 200 educators indicated only 35 percent of educators believed their schools' teachers had a high or very high comfort level connecting data to instruction; only 48 percent believed their current assessments clearly categorized which students were on track in performance vs. which required more attention; only 54 percent believed their schools' teachers have assessment data that indicates whether intervention plans are working; and only 37 percent believed their assessment data indicated how they could alter ineffective intervention plans currently in place (Andrist, 2015; eSchool News, 2015). These statistics relate to just a handful of educator needs not being met by many data report suites.

These tables were addressed in the last section:

- "Sample Data Types to Support Educators' Data Analyses" showing 333 data *types*, which contain even more actual *pieces* of data (remember this is not an exhaustive list);
- "Sample Questions Educators Want to Answer with a Data System" containing 183 questions educators might use their data system to answer after forgoing questions their data system likely cannot answer (remember this is not an exhaustive list).

Let those two tables remind us of the conundrum we are trying to tackle for our data system and the educators who use it:

> How can a data system's reports address all of educators' key questions/theories/topics, and how can it do so in a way that is user-friendly and not overwhelming?

Needs Matrix

A *needs matrix* organizes educators' data analysis needs into types, around which report designs can be constructed in order to maximize report efficiency and offer reports in a streamlined, user-friendly manner.

In addition to following other recommendations in this book, the answer lies in a needs matrix. A needs matrix organizes key educator analysis needs into types, around which report designs can be constructed. Such a matrix is featured on the next two pages.

Content Standards

Table 8.2

NEEDS MATRIX	REPORT TOPIC & SAMPLE INVESTIGATIONS SUPPORTED		FORMAT		
	Report Topic (Can Be Modified for Title, Possibly with Format Added) Sample Data Investigations Report Type Can Be Used to Address: - Sample Question Formula - Sample Question - Sample Theory		Entities	Measures/Datasets	Years/Times
Correlation (Includes Predictive)	**1-to-1 Correlation** How does/did _ affect or correlate with _? How do student grades correlate with standardized assessment performance? Mobility decreases students' sense of belonging at our school.		Single	Multiple	Single
	1-to-1 Correlation Change How (and to what extent) will/did changing _ impact _? Will improving stuc. reading skills positively affect their perform. in core courses & state+local assessments? Participation in after-school intervention will improve graduation status.		Single	Multiple	Multiple
	Correlation Identification What other characteristics do _ share? What characteristics do graduating students share? Teachers who leave the district within 3 years are mostly 1st-time teachers.		Single	Multiple	Varies
	Correlation Change Indentification What has been associated with improved _? What can our school do to improve student discipline? Implementing a stronger discipline policy & Sat. School correlated with reduced staff attrition in our school.		Single	Multiple	Multiple
Focus	**Entity's Measure Focus** How did _ perform on the _ measurement tool? How many GATE students are enrolled in school this year? On the mid-year survey, parents indicated low confidence in school safety.		Single	Single	Single
	Entity's Measure Focus How did _ perform in the area of _? How our 4th grade group perform in writing on all of this year's measures? My RSP students are entering my classroom without higher-order thinking skills.		Single	Multiple	Single
Breakdown	**Entity's Measure Breakdown** How did _ respond to each _ on the _ tool/assessment/survey/etc.? How did my class respond to each question on the End of Year Survey? Alotta struggled more with Qs at the end of the test than the beginning.		Single	Single	Single
	Multiple Entities' Measure Breakdown How did each _ respond to each _ on the _ tool/assessment/survey/etc.? How did my 8th grade class periods answer high Bloom's level Qs on last yr.'s BM4 test? As I debrief the exam's Qs with my class, each seating group will have at least 1 stud. who answered Q right.		Multiple	Single	Single
Overview	**Entity's Multiple Measure Overview** How did _ perform on these many measurement tools: _? Did Khan struggle more on the portfolio assessments than on the tests? The intervention program is going strong when it comes to assignments.		Single	Multiple	Varies
	Entity's Multiple Area Overview How did _ perform in these many areas: _? Is my child ready to apply for (and get into) a UC-level college? When I look at the dashboard I will see our school's 7th grade class is strongest in all core subjects.		Single	Multiple	Varies
Comparison (Includes Ranking & Gaps)	**Multiple Entities' Measure Comparison** How did each _ perform on the _ measurement tool? How do students' reading skills vary within each of my class periods? Some socio-ec. levels have a higher proportion of students below grade level on the LP exam than others.		Multiple	Single	Single
	Multiple Entities' Area Comparison How did each _ perform in the area of _? How do our schools compare in Writing, according to our district's various writing measures? Our lower grades are stronger in reading than the higher grades.		Multiple	Multiple	Single
Comparison (Continued)	**Multiple Entities' Multiple Measure Comparison** How did each _ perform on these many measurement tools: _? What are my son's final exam scores in each class? Some subgroups have a higher proportion of students performing below grade level in ELA than others.		Multiple	Multiple	Varies
	Multiple Entities' Multiple Area Comparison How did each _ perform in these many areas: _? What does my class roster look like and what are each student's general needs? I have at least 5 EL students in 3rd period, and they all have low scores in ELA.		Multiple	Multiple	Varies
Criteria (Includes Predictive)	**Fit Criteria Identification** What _ fit the criteria of _? Which students are at risk of dropping out? There are at least 35 students on the Honor Roll.		Varies	Varies	Single
	Requirement Fulfillment What are the answers/data for specific Qs/requests coming from _? What can I turn in as my SARC? My ELSSA Report will look like...		Single	Multiple	Multiple

197

Content Standards

Table 8.2 continued

Change (Including Growth, Can Be Cohort or Year-to-Year)	**Entity's Measure Change** How did _ change over the course of _ years/times on the _ measurement tool? How many retained kids went up a level on the state Math test? Trig's math students grew more in Number Sense than other domains on the district final.	Single	Single	Multiple
	Entity's Area Change How did _ change over the course of _ years/times in the area of _? How did high-referral students improve in perception of school? The Science Dept. had growth in hypothesis-crafting between Quarters 1 & 3.	Single	Varies	Multiple
	Entity's Multiple Measure Change How did _ change over the course of _ years/times on these many measurement tools: _? How did 1st year teachers at Will Wynn Elem. School change in their survey feedback by year end? The sites reached more of their SMART Goals this year than they did last year.	Single	Multiple	Multiple
	Entity's Multiple Area Change How did _ change over the course of _ years/times in these many areas: _? Did students noted as at-risk improve in college/career readiness? The site improved in most areas of the Health Kids Survey.	Single	Varies	Multiple
	Multiple Entities' Measure Change How did each _ change over the course of _ years/times on the _ measurement tool? How have last year's intervention students improved in reading? More Hispanic students than Asian students improved in word analysis.	Multiple	Single	Multiple
	Multiple Entities' Area Change How did each _ change over the course of _ years/times in the area of _? How many lowest-performing stud. on last yr.'s vocab exams improved in word analysis this yr.? Grade 7 made more progress in number sense than other grades did.	Multiple	Varies	Multiple
	Multiple Entities' Multiple Measure Change How did each _ change over the course of _ years/times on these many measurement tools: _? How did each department improve its integration of varied technologies? Each of my class period's students improved in word analysis.	Multiple	Multiple	Multiple
Position	**Position on Continuum** What is _'s position in the numerous ranked areas of the _ standards/rubric/scales? At which grade level is Paige performing on each of the CCSS ELA standards? Skip scored lower on the writing rubric categories related to style and voice than he did on mechanics.	Single	Single	Multiple

---

Aspects of the Needs Matrix

(Explaining Example Above)

Terms Used in Matrix

Entities See bulleted examples in the *Entity* section, below.

Measures/Datasets A single measure or dataset means one test's scores, one evaluation's marks, one survey's responses, one demographics set, etc.; multiple measures/datasets would mean data from multiple sources, such as multiple tests' scores, multiple evaluations' marks, etc.

Years/Times This relates to the number of years' (or time periods, such as quarters) data is displayed for each measure/dataset and does not relate to the academic/enrollment year (which may be the same as or different from the measure/dataset year).

Topics Absorbed by Reports

Criterion-Based Growth Allow users to easily set criteria-based groups (e.g., run a fit list report or other means of generating a list of students, then save those students as a group such as "students with 10+ truancies and 5+ detentions"), then have the ability to select the group with reports' input controls to generate reports with this group as the selected entity. Thus this topic does not require additional reports, as it can be absorbed by other reports.

Cohort vs. Year-to-Year Growth Allow users to select different year combinations (e.g., enrollment year vs. testing year) in order to report on a cohort *or* non-cohort basis.

When Running Each of These Reports

Entity Though not charted, when running any of the reports listed in the needs matrix the user should have the ability to opt (through input control) to generate the report for one (and ideally each) of these entity levels:

- Student
- Program/Group
- Class Period
- Course
- Department
- Teacher
- Grade Level
- School
- District
- Similar School
- County
- State

Combos The ability to select combinations of entities or criteria is also helpful. For example, you might want to select a *Teacher* and *Grade Level* (e.g., to show only the results of teacher Anita Book's 7th grade students).

Audience and Format Though not charted, when running any of the reports listed in the needs matrix the user should have the ability to generate the report topic for one (and nearly each) of these formats, which each have a version geared toward one audience (or a combination, as is sometimes appropriate for parent/student):

Format	Educator	Parent	Student	(same version for Parent/Stud.)
List	X			
Snapshot	X	X	X	X
Description	X			
Seating	X			
Rubric	X	X	X	
Grouping	X		X	
Schedule	X	X	X	X
Calendar	X	X	X	X
Letter	X	X	X	
Slip	X		X	

It is usually appropriate for the format to form the last word of the report's title. It is also appropriate for some formats to end with a snapshot.

Format Descriptions

List Each entity is listed in a row with data.

Snapshot Often one page, a collection of graphs gives a summary/overview.

Description Heavy text is accommodated, such as lengthy survey Q&A.

Seating Results are displayed in a way that matches the class seating chart.

Rubric Results are shown within the context of a rubric's levels and criteria.

Grouping A teacher can see suggested groupings for differentiation, and a student can see all of his or her groups for various standards or activities.

Schedule The most common example is the class schedule.

Calendar Calendar format can juxtapose data (such as performance data) with information like a curriculum pacing guide, attendance, work completion, etc.

200

> **Letter** A letter combines user-friendly explanation with data.
>
> **Slip** Multiple slips print per page, allowing teachers to efficiently cut/hand out data that is specific to each student (e.g., each student's own test results print).

No Gaps

One of the key reasons for a needs matrix is to avoid reporting gaps. Reporting gaps occur when one or both of the following occurs:

- Key, needed data analyses are not facilitated by any reports in the report suite.
- Key, needed data analyses can only be accommodated when reports and/or features not intended for those analyses have to be used (e.g., in a cumbersome way) because no better alternatives exist in the report suite.

By building a report suite around a needs matrix like the one shown earlier in this chapter's "Organized to Cover Needs Matrix" section, such gaps are significantly reduced or largely eliminated. However, to achieve this, the report suite must not only adhere to the needs matrix, but must also follow other OTCD Standards for good design. The DSRP will want to consciously design the preplanned reports to avoid reporting gaps.

Note this involves avoiding major gaps in report audience. Though many reports will be appropriate for multiple stakeholders, be sure there are not cases where appropriate versions of reports are not available for stakeholders who need them. For example, students need to know how they are progressing in varied areas over time, so it would be a problem if none of the reports that show progress were communicated in student-friendly ways.

Report audience also relates to comfort levels when using data. Though you should never (ever!) simplify a report to the point that the data's true meaning is lost, consider "Lite" versions of reports that communicate smaller portions of other reports' contents. Adding the word "Lite" to the end of each of these report titles lets users know a more elaborate version is available when they are ready.

Though not as dire a problem as reporting gaps, adhering to a needs matrix also helps the report suite to avoid unnecessary redundancy. Reporting redundancy occurs when many reports serve relatively the same purpose, only with slight variations. In some cases this requires users to run each of a series of reports to achieve a purpose when it would have been more efficient to run one report that offered all key data a user needed. Redundancy contributes to clutter in a report suite, which makes the suite harder and more time-intensive to navigate.

Topic-Focused (e.g., Topic-Titled)

Earlier in this book (for Standards 1.1.05, 4.4.03, 4.5.01, and 5.2.03) we looked at reasons it is unproductive to tie each report (e.g., exclusively, as indicated by its title) to a single test or measurement. Unfortunately, there is a discrepancy between most data system report titles (e.g., test-exclusive) and recommended approaches to data investigation (e.g., investigating a question, theory, or topic).

In this chapter we have established each report should not be tied to a single question or theory (e.g., question-titled or theory-titled) due to the infinite number of questions and theories per report. Since investigating a question, theory, or topic are the three most common recommended approaches (and good approaches) to educator data investigation, this leaves topic-focused (e.g., topic-titled) as a remaining possibility. Fortunately, it is a good option.

Using topic-based titles such as those featured on the sample needs matrix also facilitates other best practices promoted by OTCD Standards. For example, topic-titled reports keep a report list to a manageable size while still allowing for multiple variations (e.g., via input controls) and for variation-based searches (e.g., using a test's title as a filter to find all reports accommodating that test's results).

Region-Specific

Many DSRPs have clients in different states or regions, and so the data system report contents to which clients have access should vary by region (as covered in the "Audience-Appropriate" section of this chapter). While the contents within reports are tied to region, so is the report suite as a whole.

Namely, as a DSRP you should ensure the varying reports required for each client region (and thus the varying reports available) cover the entire needs matrix for every client region. For example, if a particular region lacks an assessment other regions use to address some topics within the needs matrix, the DSRP and educator should strive to find another way to address those topics with the client's existing or potential data. Otherwise, some students will not have the same access to data-informed assistance as students in other regions.

References

Andrist, C. (2015, July 15). *New survey from Lexia Learning shows educators struggle with translating screener assessment data into actionable plans.* Retrieved from http://lexialearning.com/success/press-releases/lexia-survey-assessment (accessed October 30, 2015).

Davis, M. R. (2013, October 1). Managing the digital district: Intelligent data analysis helps predict needs. *Education Week*, 33(06), 20–21. Bethesda, MD: Editorial Projects in Education.

eSchool News (2015, July 16). Informal survey suggests disconnect between teachers and data. *eSchool News*. Retrieved from www.eschoolnews.com/2015/07/16/teachers-data-142 (accessed October 30, 2015).

Kenny, D. (2010). DataToText: A consumer-oriented approach to data analysis. *Multivariate Behavioral Research*, 45(6), 1000–1019. doi:10.1080/00273171. 2010.531232

Tally, S. (2013, September 25). Purdue software boosts graduation rate 21 percent. *Purdue News*. West Lafayette, IN: Purdue University.

U.S. Department of Education Office of Educational Technology (2012). *Enhancing teaching and learning through educational data mining and learning analytics: An issue brief.* Washington, DC: Author.

U.S. Department of Education Office of Planning, Evaluation and Policy Development (2011). *Teachers' ability to use data to inform instruction: Challenges and supports.* United States Department of Education (ERIC Document Reproduction Service No. ED516494).

9 | **Work with Educators**

Communication

Once, as a district administrator, I was in the middle of conducting a training session at our district office on how to use our data and assessment management system to construct a benchmark test. Teacher and principal representatives from every school in our district were present, each attendee had a set of lesson handouts I had prepared that would walk them through each step during or after the training session, and I knew everything I had to cover during the session. Then, right in the middle of the session, the entire assessment-building interface swapped to a completely new (and hard to figure out) way of building assessments in the system.

None of us at the district office—or anywhere else in the district—had received any advanced warning the system would change, let alone change in such a dramatic way. Imagine how this lack of warning from our DSRP affected the training, educators' time, educators' willingness and ability to use the system, etc. Imagine what this experience did to our district's relationship with the DSRP. It was very damaging. In fact, we dropped the vendor and switched to a new DSRP the following year.

If you are a DSRP who provides data tools to educators, you need to keep key educator leaders in the loop of changes, enhancements, problems, or any other information that will impact their data use. Likewise, you should be regularly listening to your clients to help determine what those changes and enhancements will be, and to hear about any problems you need to remedy. If you are a within-district educator providing data tools to staff, you will want to be equally diligent keeping educators informed of what resources they can expect and when.

Work with Educators

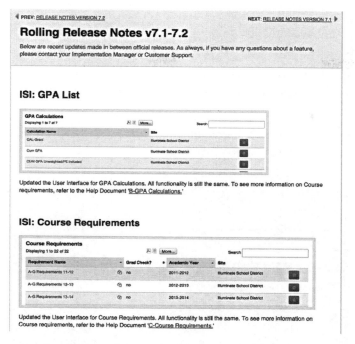

Figure 9.1 Excerpt from Illuminate Education Release Notes

Lane Rankin, CEO/Founder of Illuminate Education, enlists and recommends the following strategies for keeping users informed:

- Every time a new product version is released, release notes (sample excerpt shown in Figure 9.1) are written to summarize key changes and enhancements, and these explanations are paired with links to related help lessons. The release notes are emailed to key district contacts and can be redistributed as each district desires. All users can also access these release notes when they log into the system, and can explore any past release notes anytime within the help system.
- Implementation managers reach out to district contacts prior to big releases to help districts prepare for any major changes, or to highlight changes in which the districts were particularly interested.
- Illuminate hosts regular (e.g., monthly or quarterly) regional user meetings any users may attend, such as at the local county departments of education.

Work with Educators

- A quarterly newsletter showcases a current user each quarter, sharing special ways in which that customer uses Illuminate and other helpful news.
- Free webinars are offered to better acquaint users with system features and best practices. Anyone who registers may attend these webinars online.
- The company posts announcements on the data system's login screen and updates them weekly.

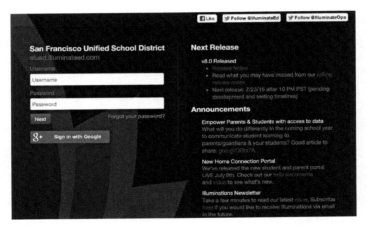

Figure 9.2 Illuminate Education Login Screen Features Announcements and Access to Release Notes

- The company runs an annual user conference in key locations, where thousands of users each select and attend sessions that suit their interests. A roadmap of the upcoming year's enhancement plans is shared at a "Future of Illuminate" session for all attendees.
- Social media is leveraged. Two staff members are charged with using a designated Twitter account (which interested users can follow) to tweet system updates, new release announcements, and other news that impacts product use. This account is not cluttered with promotional news or research; rather, it simply covers operations.
- The Illuminate Education Blog will be launched in 2016 as a space where thought leaders outside of and within the company can write about current education topics relevant to the product's users.

Work with Educators

- A warm, collaborative relationship between client and company is paramount. Each client is assigned an Illuminate Implementation Manager who takes special care of that client's interests.

If you are a DSRP on a smaller scale—such as an educator who regularly builds data reports for your colleagues—your communication with data users will likely be less formal. You can help this relationship by being readily available for those who use your reports, such as to answer questions, assist in use of the reports, or listen to staff's additional data needs.

Real World Implementation: A Message for Vendors

By Rufus Thompson, Implementation Manager at Illuminate Education and Former Technology Coordinator for Mountain View School District in Ontario, California

Bridging the gap between the *perceived* and *actual* capability of clients is an ongoing challenge when training and supporting school and district staffs. Those who have an aptitude for technology will not have a problem with the technology but may have a problem with the interface that the technology displays. Vendors have attempted to provide user-friendly interfaces once the user lands in their system via a web browser. This careful site design eliminates the need to know how to use the browser because the commands to navigate the system are executed within the browser window.

District and school leadership facilitate success when training staff. If the leadership supports the goals of the ongoing training of all users, the goals of the training are much easier to achieve because users know the goals are universal. The goals should always ultimately focus on student success. The student is the client of the education system; the data system facilitates his or her needs by empowering the users of that system. The more clean and useful the data provided for each student are, the greater the likelihood that decision makers in the classroom, school, and district level will make life-changing decisions, which include day-to-day well-informed data-driven decisions.

Teachers are often the largest user-base and have a lot to do by the very nature of their jobs. There is sometimes a disconnect between teachers and those in Information Technology positions. The Information Technology folks sometimes think teachers cannot work effectively with data. Does this sound familiar? This is a mindset that many teachers have about students in their classroom regarding achievement.

Students are the benefactors of the decisions of properly prepared users who interpret the data in the data system and create action plans for students. This often means going beyond the interface to mindset work about the student populations being served.

In summary, here are some things vendors can do to make their systems work best for educators:

- Provide an accurate and clear picture of the implementation process.
- Provide Technical Support in many forms for the client and allow any user to use that Tech Support.
- Forge an ongoing and lasting relationship with all stakeholders.
- Provide professional development for all users.
- Continue to refresh and enhance the product.
- Make the user experience and the data easy to use and effective to present in reports.
- Accept input from clients to make their experience better.
- Focus on the ultimate goal, which is making a student's life better.

Respect Data Users' Expertise

Just as you want the educator to respect your expertise in technology and data, as well as your expertise in working with a large number of school districts, you must respect the educator's expertise. Educators have vast stores of knowledge and experience in specialized areas that impact data use and data needs. In addition, each school district will have a unique set of priorities due to its unique demographics, its unique staff, and other factors.

Work with Educators

Anyone communicating directly with educator users must be able to listen well and respect what the educator is saying. When both sides work together to pursue what is best for the system, you will all have the advantage of both sides' expertise.

Troubleshooting

Poor communication can extend the time and resources it takes to fix problems within the data system. When clients report problems, garner specifics from them concerning what is wrong. You might provide them with suggested guidelines such as these (note the easy-for-anyone-to-understand language) for reporting a problem to your organization:

- Provide a screenshot of the area in the data system where the problem appears. The table below will help you take a screenshot, which involves saving a picture of what your screen looks like so you can send that picture file to us.

Table 9.1

Computer	How to Take a Screenshot
Mac	On your keyboard, simultaneously press *Command* (⌘), *Shift*, and *3*. This will save (to your desktop) a screenshot of everything you see on your computer screen. To save an image of just a portion of your screen, simultaneously press *Command* (⌘), *Shift*, and *4*, then select a screen area using your mouse.
Windows	On your keyboard, simultaneously press *Ctrl*, *Alt*, and *Print Screen* (sometimes abbreviated as *Prtsc*). This will save a screenshot to your clipboard, which you can then paste in a program like Microsoft Word by simultaneously pressing *Ctrl* and *V* on your keyboard. Save that file by simultaneously pressing *Ctrl* and *S* on your keyboard.
Windows (newer editions, such as Windows 7)	On your screen, click *Start* and then type snipping in the search field. All Programs. Click *Snipping Tool* when you see it appear at the top of the window. Click (and hold down your click) to select the part of the screen you want to save. When you let go, you can click *File* and then *Save As* within the Snipping Tool window to save your screenshot.

209

- Describe where the problem occurs in the data system (it sometimes helps to provide the URL that appears when you are on a specific screen). The following table will show you how to take a screenshot, which is a savable image of what you are seeing on your computer screen.

- Explain what you see in the data system vs. what you need to see and why (e.g., what you are trying to achieve, or how the current function impacts data use).

- If the problem involves an action, describe the current process (e.g., what you are clicking, step by step).

- Provide any examples or details to help the DSRP spot the problem (e.g., "If you generate the 2015 *Class Roster* report for teacher *Kurt Lecture* at *Earl. E. Learner Elementary*, notice how student *Val A. Dictorian* shows 105 percent for attendance when such a record is not possible").

A "Lean in" Culture

When product development involves input from varied stakeholders—such as principals, programmers, etc.—the product will typically be better. Any dialogue concerning communication between entities in (or across) work environments can be more honest and more helpful by acknowledging equity issues.

It should go without saying that everyone involved in a report suite's improvement should give equal merit to others' input regardless of race, culture, creed, age, etc. when educators and DSRPs converse and—at times—disagree. However, given the significant gender differences prevalent between data system users/educators (disproportionately female) and data system DSRPs (disproportionately male), the gender issues are especially relevant to making education data reports and systems that work:

- **Educators**—Data systems' leading consumers are female; the U.S. Dept. of Education's National Center for Education Statistics reports 75 percent of all teachers are women (Papay, Harvard Graduate School of Education, 2007).

Work with Educators

- **DSRPs**—Only 22 percent of computer programmers and 21 percent of computer software engineers (i.e., the roles commonly involved in building reports in education data systems) are female (U.S. Department of Labor, U.S. Bureau of Labor Statistics, 2011).

It is strongly recommended all parties intimately involved with the report suite read Sheryl Sandberg's *Lean In* (at least chapters 1–3 and 10) or similar literature to refresh and expand their understanding of current gender issues impacting their communication. Discussion should ensue, as should deliberate and active steps to best ensure the gender differences common in DSRP/educator correspondence do not undermine the data system's reflection of educator and researcher input.

Before you skip this, note:

- both genders contribute to this issue; and
- those who feel they demonstrate no gender bias can actually be *more* likely to demonstrate gender bias due to what's known as a "bias blind spot" (Sandberg, 2013).

Many development and reporting debacles occur with data systems because of miscommunication between educators and DSRPs: some because a voice was misunderstood, and some because a voice was never fully heard in the first place. This even occurs when the women concerned work for the DSRP. Whether district-based or an outside vendor, the DSRP seeks to provide a product to best help educators, but often this desire is not fully reflected in what the DSRP ultimately produces, and it is likely gender bias plays a role in many subtle ways.

Both genders can take steps to improve communication between educators and edtech, regardless of the side on which they work, as well as within their own workplaces. Reading a book such as *Lean In* can help tremendously in this regard.

Of course, everyone's voice ought to be heard, regardless of gender or role. Women have certainly been known to undervalue men, and an educator who undervalues a DSRP can certainly push for a reporting change that is technically undesirable. Given statistics regarding the typical gender composition disparity between the education and edtech fields, as well as statistics indicating the more common suppressions of the female

211

voice in professional environments, however, this section merits special consideration by this book's audience, male and female alike. Thus, despite the stigma attached to talking about this issue, I am choosing to talk about it. I hope you will, too.

References

Papay, J., Harvard Graduate School of Education (2007). *Aspen Institute datasheet: The teaching workforce.* Washington, DC: The Aspen Institute.

Sandberg, S. (2013). *Lean in: Women, work, and the will to lead.* New York, NY: Alfred A. Knopf.

U.S. Department of Labor, U.S. Bureau of Labor Statistics (2011, July). *Highlights of women's earnings in 2010: Report 1031.* Retrieved from www.bls.gov/cps/cpswom2010.pdf (accessed October 30, 2015).

10 | Put It All Together

"Big Picture" Action Table

> **Resources**
>
> Access the following:
> - Big Picture Action Table
> - All OTCD Standards
> - Details on research-based evidence supporting OTCD Standards

As you implement standards, you will likely need to communicate with others who do not necessarily have your same level of understanding of data, education, and/or technology. Back up requests and communication with resources that can bridge the understanding gap (e.g., a state's data analysis guidelines for a particular test, an article on how personalized learning works, an annotated screenshot showing what you are seeing on a data system page vs. what you should be seeing, etc.). The Big Picture Action Table communicates some actions and considerations that can help as you take steps to implement this book's standards, based on whatever your overarching circumstances may be.

Help for the Overwhelmed

While reading this book, you likely identified many areas in your report environment that need improvement, as well as many next steps you hope to take to produce needed improvements. Online tools for evaluating your data system and/or reports can help you in this endeavor. If you feel overwhelmed, these tips can help:

Standards that Make the Biggest Difference

Consider which standards will be most effective in improving data use, and for which areas. For example, if your district coordinators report staff members are regularly drawing false conclusions from data when using a particular report, concentrate efforts on solving problems for this particular report (e.g., create a reference sheet for the report, add a footer to the report, change the report's design or submit a request that its design be changed, etc.).

Standards that Are Easiest to Implement

Some standards will be easier for you to implement than others, based on your unique circumstances, such as:

- your staff resources where report creation is concerned;
- your data system's technological ability to accommodate a standard;
- your team's openness to change;
- your team's ability to work together;
- your clients' willingness to work with you.

Determine which standards are:

- most within your control and ability to implement;
- easiest/fastest for you to implement.

Then consider starting with those standards. You can even enlist a combination of approaches, such as initiating changes for important-yet-hard-to-implement standards (e.g., standards for which you can only do so much and have to wait on someone to fully implement), and then implementing easy-to-do standards while you await the other standards' completion.

Users as Collaborators

Leverage good relations with your users to collaborate in areas where educational expertise is needed. For example:

- One district might have a tech coordinator who has produced "help sheets" for using the technology. With this person's and district's consent, you could copy/paste the text from these sheets into technology help lessons.
- One district might have a data coach who has produced a reference sheet to accompany each of your most popular data reports. With this person's and district's consent, you could turn these sheets into reference sheets housed within your data system.

While the above examples relate to existing resources, your clients might be willing to work with you on new resources that can benefit them as well as others. Such collaboration typically reduces your workload and improves the quality of the resources.

Final Words

Imagine data that is easy for educators to understand and use, because:

- You provide data systems/reports that adhere to best practices for reporting data to educators (i.e., data is "over-the-counter" and thus easy to understand and use); and
- the educators provide a data use climate that supports staff and the ongoing professional development and guidance data users need.

In this scenario, both edtech providers and educator leaders have done what is in their power to make data easy to use and understand. Making data work for educators takes a team effort, and students suffer if either side drops the ball.

Now imagine an environment that does not offer such assistance. Think of the impact this book's concepts have on data-using educators and—most importantly—students impacted by data-informed decisions. Remember research indicating most educators are analyzing data incorrectly when using typical data reports (which do not usually adhere to this book's standards).

As you take steps outlined in this book, encourage dialogue about making data easy for educators. Share this book with others in the education, edtech, and research communities and discuss its implications as new developments in these communities arise. Note *How to Make Data Work: A Guide for Educational Leaders*, by Dr. Jenny Grant Rankin, is a companion book to the one you are reading and concerns how educators can help, as well.

Remember:

- Fewer than half of educators' data analyses (using typical, hard-to-understand reports) are accurate, despite the benefits of traditional interventions such as PD and staffing-based supports.
- Educators comprise a favorable user-base and are not to blame for most poor data use.
- Educators' data misunderstandings directly impact students.
- Making data work for educators by following the standards in this book has been shown to improve educators' data analyses by up to 436 percent (Rankin, 2013).

As DSRPs, we are entrusted with the care of kids' lives. Students are at our mercy and it is our job to do the best we can to help them. If you are a DSRP, I assume you share this goal. If you are a DSRP, I imagine you cannot decline this chance to see gains such as 436 percent that ultimately affect students. I know you can use this book to make data work for educators and other stakeholders, and I trust that you will.

Reference

Rankin, J. G. (2013). *Over-the-counter data's impact on educators' data analysis accuracy.* ProQuest Dissertations and Theses, 3575082. Retrieved from http://pqdtopen.proquest.com/doc/1459258514.html?FMT=ABS (accessed October 30, 2015).

Helping you to choose the right eBooks for your Library

Add Routledge titles to your library's digital collection today. Taylor and Francis ebooks contains over 50,000 titles in the Humanities, Social Sciences, Behavioural Sciences, Built Environment and Law.

Choose from a range of subject packages or create your own!

Benefits for you
- Free MARC records
- COUNTER-compliant usage statistics
- Flexible purchase and pricing options
- All titles DRM-free.

Benefits for your user
- Off-site, anytime access via Athens or referring URL
- Print or copy pages or chapters
- Full content search
- Bookmark, highlight and annotate text
- Access to thousands of pages of quality research at the click of a button.

REQUEST YOUR FREE INSTITUTIONAL TRIAL TODAY

Free Trials Available
We offer free trials to qualifying academic, corporate and government customers.

eCollections – Choose from over 30 subject eCollections, including:

Archaeology	Language Learning
Architecture	Law
Asian Studies	Literature
Business & Management	Media & Communication
Classical Studies	Middle East Studies
Construction	Music
Creative & Media Arts	Philosophy
Criminology & Criminal Justice	Planning
Economics	Politics
Education	Psychology & Mental Health
Energy	Religion
Engineering	Security
English Language & Linguistics	Social Work
Environment & Sustainability	Sociology
Geography	Sport
Health Studies	Theatre & Performance
History	Tourism, Hospitality & Events

For more information, pricing enquiries or to order a free trial, please contact your local sales team:
www.tandfebooks.com/page/sales

The home of Routledge books

www.tandfebooks.com